# DIGITAL LIBRARY BASICS

## A PRACTICAL MANUAL

# DIGITAL LIBRARY BASICS

## A PRACTICAL MANUAL

K. RAJASEKARAN
R. RAMAN NAIR
K M. NAFALA

**Ess Ess Publications**
New Delhi

***Digital Library Basics***
***A Practical Manual***



**ISBN: 978-81-7000-601-5**

**Rs.600/-**

**First Published 2010**

Published by:
**Ess Ess Publications**
4837/24, Ansari Road,
Darya Ganj,
New Delhi-110 002.
INDIA
Phones: 23260807, 41563444
Fax: 41563334
E-mail: info@essessreference.com
www.essessreference.com

Cover Design by *Patch Creative Unit*

Printed and bound in India at Salasar Imaging Systems.

# CONTENTS

CONTENTS

CONTENTS

# PREFACE

Libraries are everywhere undergoing transformation, especially owing to the developments in Information and Communication Technologies (ICT). Traditional libraries are changing to digital libraries and new libraries that are being set up are increasingly of the digital kind. This results in a widespread interest in Digital Library and Archive development. In India many institutions are in the process of setting up digital libraries and archives.

India is rich in various kinds of traditional knowledge. This heritage is partially documented in various forms and is available in museums, archives and libraries. Even old small college libraries and village libraries as well as private collections in families contain rare and unique documents with knowledge or information not otherwise available. Beyond this there is also knowledge that rarely gets formally documented. They consist of knowledge that is orally transmitted inside families, ritualistic art forms specifically limited to a geographical area, or agricultural or medical techniques and combinations used in remote village or by tribal groups. Tracing out such records and knowledge by major projects from distant locations or government cannot yield good result. Local initiatives are important and their coordination can give magical effect in conserving our knowledge heritage. With digital library technology and tools, it is possible not only to document, archive and conserve such knowledge resources for posterity at the local level but also to replicate and disseminate such information to the world with ease. Normally local initiatives cannot afford complicated and costly solutions meant for digital libraries and archive development.

Digital Libraries and Archives are organized collections of documents in digital form. They may contain documents in different formats ranging from manuscripts, diaries, letters, books, research papers, reports, newspapers, periodicals, photographs, maps, video tapes, audio files, etc. Collecting organizing and managing them in a retrievable way and providing access to them from distant locations needs hardware and software solutions meant for that.

Open Access movement has made digitization important due to its power to extend access. Understanding the need for open access to knowledge resources; open source software movement, free software movement etc have created many digital library and institutional repository software.

Digital library software programs like the WINISIS/GenISIS, Greenstone, DSpace, EPrints etc have hastened the digital library/archive creation process. Libraries are today playing a lead role in the creation of institutional repositories supporting the cause of Open Access.

This manual is intended to introduce the application of free software tools developed by UNESCO with the objective to empower the users by giving them access to key technology for development and knowledge sharing, that most of them otherwise cannot afford. The main objective of UNESCO is to build a knowledge society based on the sharing of knowledge and incorporating all the socio-cultural and ethical dimensions of sustainable development. With these objective UNESCO has developed various standards and management tools, to strengthen libraries and archives as key actors in knowledge societies, and for fostering access at the community level.

UNESCO packages are developed in a way in which they can enable librarians, scientists and others with minimum computer awareness to plan, assemble, develop and manage small or large digital libraries and archives. So any local communities or even families having record collections can use them with ease.

This manual explains without technical jargon the methods for developing and managing Digital Archives, Digital Libraries and e-Document collections using WINISIS and GenISIS, making them accessible with search mechanisms over Intranet/Internet using GenISISWEB, publishing them with search engine in CDROMs using GenISISCD; and also converting such collections to Greenstone for publication in the Web or in CDROM. This manual can help to create electronic publications with search and full text retrieval facility and launch Digital Libraries/Archives of full text, image, audio and video files, accessible over the Web using free software developed by UNESCO.

This manual was originally prepared for use in informal training programmes conducted by Centre for Agricultural Informatics for small groups from local governments and agricultural organizations. It was further developed for using at the International Workshop on UNESCO 's WINISIS/GenISIS conducted by Mahatma Gandhi University at Kuttikkanam in Kerala during 2008. Suggestions provided by Ms. R. Sujatha, Ms. Laila T Abraham, Mr. Sebastian Joseph, Ms. N. Deepa and Mr. S P. Sunny from MG University and Mr. Jobin Jose of Marian

College; members of the organizing team and Dr. Adebambo A Oduwole, Mr. Evanson Nedungu and Mr. Teddy N Alias participants of the workshop helped immensely to finalize the present version of the manual. Users are requested to sent their comments and suggestions to cagiindia@gmail.com

# 1 DIGITAL LIBRARIES

Digital library development requires computers and application software meant for different processes related to digitization. The software used for these functions are highly specialized ones which are not familiar to general computer users. This chapter will discuss the minimum hardware and software requirements for establishing a small digitization lab for archiving local collections or selected small collections of books and image, audio and video documents.

# DIGITAL LIBRARIES

## DIGITAL ARCHIVES AND LIBRARIES

Digital libraries and archives can provide access to information 'on demand' regardless of location of the computer or other storage devices in which documents are kept. Here we will discuss the main characteristics of digital libraries and archives.

The term 'archives' denotes public records or historical documents, or the place where such records and documents are kept. The term 'library' also invokes in our mind a storehouse of information in the form of print on paper publications like books, journals, reports, etc. and newer media such as films, filmstrips, video and audio cassettes. Most of us view the library as a place where such information 'containers' are acquired, organized, shelved and retrieved. More-recently, many archives, libraries and information centers have begun to use online database search systems and connections to the Online Public Access Catalogues (OPACs) of other libraries, over telecommunication networks. Many libraries have also taken advantage of CD-ROM technology to provide users network access to large information bases. With such remote information access, the physical location of the library has become irrelevant.

The way we view information sources is changing due to the emergence of global computer networks. Personal computers are now usually part of a network of computers and often part of a network of networks, spanning the globe. Until recently, computers and computer networks were accessible easily only to a privileged few - computer scientists, researchers and hobbyists. For the common people they were out of reach, economically and practically. Now, computers have become less expensive and inter connectivity is much more widespread. People are becoming more computer literate, and systems are becoming simpler and more accessible. These are changing the way we communicate and how we think about libraries and information.

The Internet and the World Wide Web (WWW) technologies are providing the technological environment and intellectual impetus for the development of 'digital libraries' -libraries without walls, with container less data and ideas. The Internet has enabled global connectivity of computers and the development of various tools and techniques for networked information provision and access. Starting with basic tools like e-mail (messaging), ftp (file transfer) and telnet (remote login), the Internet has progressed to provide user-friendly tools like Gopher, WAIS and the WWW for information publishing and access. The WWW, which is integrating all other access tools, also provides a very convenient means for publishing and accessing multi media, hypertext linked documents stored in computers spread across the world, using text coding standards such as HTML and SGML. These tools have been used for providing access to a variety of information sources and services, including dictionaries and encyclopedias, electronic journals and news letters, tables of contents, preprints, technical reports, software and data archives, library catalogues, discussion forums, courseware, directories, etc. As most of the researchers have desktop computers that are connected to the Internet via Intranets they can very quickly start accessing and publishing information in the Web.

**Definition**

Digital libraries is an evolving area of research, development and application and multiple definitions have been offered by professionals in this area.

Arms define digital Libraries as managed collection of information with associated services, wherein information is stored in digital format accessible over network. Patel and Sharma defines it as a set of electronic resources and associated technical capabilities for creating searching and using information. According to Oppenheim and Stein it is an information service in which all information resources are available in computer processable form and the function of acquisition, storage, preservation, retrieval, access and display are carried out through use of digital technologies.

Based on common aspects among these definitions, digital libraries may be defined as electronic information collections containing large and diverse repositories of digital objects, which can be accessed by a large number of geographically distributed users. Such repositories would exist in locations physically near or remote from the users. Digital objects include text, images, maps, sounds, videos, catalogues and indices, and scientific, business, and government data sets as well as hyper textual multimedia compositions of such elements.

Operationally therefore, digital libraries will be network based distributed systems with individual servers responsible for maintaining local collections of digital documents ranging from sets of electronic texts to video-on-demand services. From the user's point of view, however, there should appear to be a single digital library system, integrating personal information, work group and organizational information collections and public digital libraries. Any given digital library system should therefore provide a coherent, consistent view of as many of these repositories as possible and allow users to seamlessly connect and interact with information with no regard to geographic location or time.

There is also general acceptance of the fact that digital libraries would need to span both print and digital materials. For the foreseeable future print on paper publications are expected to be around and thus digital libraries are expected to provide integrated, coherent access to both types of materials.

Digital Libraries partially or in full mirror collections and library services that exist or existed in traditional form also. A digital Library is analogous to traditional library in terms of diversity and complexity of the collection. Digital Libraries and traditional libraries are not two competing forms. Digital Library technologies will complement traditional library functions and services.

**Key Components**

Key components of digital libraries, are therefore: geographically distributed digital information collections, geographically distributed users, information represented by a variety of digital objects, large and diverse collections and seamless' access.

The schematic representation of the emerging global digital library environment is shown in figure 1.1. It shows users (desk-top computers) connected to the global network via institutional Local Area Networks (LAN) and Network Service Providers (NSP). Variety of digital information collections will be mounted on powerful workstations (DLS) in stand alone or networked configurations. Using powerful, but very user friendly browser programs similar to Internet Explorer on their desktops, users will be able to seamlessly connect to and extract information from geographically distributed digital libraries. This process will be facilitated by intelligent information finding agents that will use variety of tools like Meta databases and search engines to extract and deliver relevant information to the user's desktop.

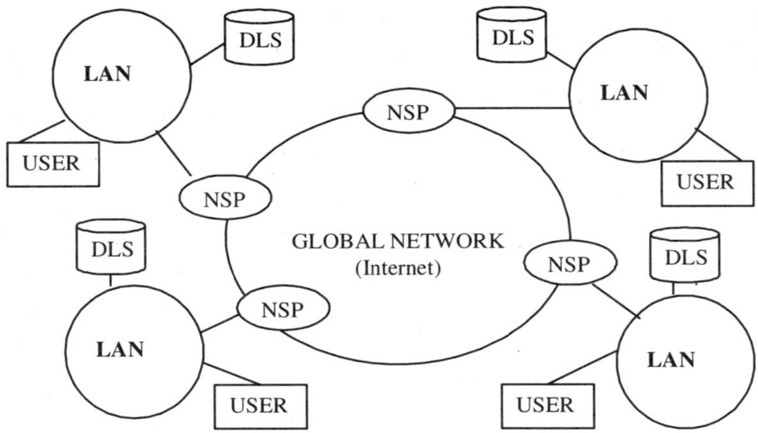


**Figure 1.1: Global Digital Library Environment**

## Digital, Electronic and Virtual Libraries:

The use of terminologies like virtual, *digital* and *electronic* libraries creates some confusion. One person's digital library is often another's virtual library. Some useful distinctions have recently been made.

Electronic library is a library that provides collection and/or services in electronic form, for example, optical video disk (which is not digital), CDROM, online, etc.

Digital library is a library that provides collection and services in digital form.

Virtual library is a library that does not physically *exist,* most often used to denote a library with distributed collections or services that appear and act as one. Typical example is a Web site with pointers and links to other sites,

From the above it may be seen that electronic library

is more inclusive than digital library. However, digital library has come to be the preferred term, perhaps keeping in line with terms like digital audio and digital video. The current usage of the term 'digital library' appears to encompass both electronic and virtual libraries.

**Advantages of Digital Libraries:**

Some of the key advantages digital libraries provide include the following:

**Ability to search:** The ability to search provides an enormous advantage to electronic materials when an ASCII version is available. Online searching has for some years been replacing printed abstract journals. Since most of the modern material is now produced via computers, it can generally be provided in ASCII form and be searched. For those documents, which are searched rather than read like reference books, compilations, etc. electronics can be expected to take over shortly. Printed encyclopedias, for example, are giving way to CDROMs, which are small, cheaper, and far more effective.

**Ubiquity:** Another key advantage is ubiquity -a single electronic copy can be accessed from numerous locations, by many simultaneous users. Copies can be delivered with electronic speed, and it would be possible to reformat the material as per the reader's preferences like character or image size etc. Since readers get a screen display of the object, rather than a physical object, loss rates by theft are eliminated in case of rare, antique or costly documents.

**Support to Wider Range of Materials:** Digital storage also permits libraries to expand the range of material they can provide to their users. Since audiocassette tapes and records cannot stand a large number of playings without deterioration, their digital representation like digital audio can produce a format that is much safer and of better quality. Digital material can also permit access to videotapes and new kinds of multi-media materials that are created only on computers and have no equivalent in any traditional format.

**Preservation:** Another major advantage is preservation. Digital information can be copied without error. As a result, preservation in a digital world does not depend on having a permanent object and keeping it under guard, but on the ability to make multiple copies, assuming that at least one will survive.

**Access to Current Information:** For researchers, digital libraries provide access to up to date current literature and thereby help them to be aware of current trends.

## Technologies for Digital Libraries

Digital libraries are considered by many to be a very challenging research area, as it requires development and integration of several highly sophisticated hardware and software technologies, and pooling together of multi-disciplinary expertise. While many of the technologies required for the development and deployment of digital libraries and their access are available today, their performance needs to be scaled up to handle very large digital collections in networked environment. It is expected that several digital library projects currently underway will result in technologies that may be used readily to develop new digital libraries.

Some of the major areas of focus are: multi-media object storage, retrieval and transmission; data compression; digitization covering multimedia data capturing and conversion; hypermedia navigation; authoring tools for creating electronic documents; multimedia object representation (e.g. HTML, SGML), meta databases, display technologies; user interfaces and search, retrieval and routing software.

**Issues in Digital Libraries**

Work in the area of digital libraries has thrown up several issues and challenges; Key issues include copyright and technological obsolescence.

**Copyright:** It is very easy to copy, replicate and distribute digital information. Enforcing copyright in digital environment is a major issue. Technological obsolescence is mainly in regard to hardware and software.

**Hardware:** The major risk to digital objects is not physical deterioration, but technological obsolescence of the devices to read them, While the lifetime of optical and magneto-optical cartridges is expected to be in decades, those of reading devices is only about one decade. Reasonable refreshing schedule and use of widely marketed devices than special purpose devices are some advisable solutions.

**Software:** A more serious problem is software obsolescence. It has been pointed out that the variety of software formats far exceeds the number of hardware devices manufactured, and that these programs come and go more quickly than the hardware does. Libraries should rely on standards like MARC and SGML, which are expected to exist for the foreseeable future.

**Cost of Regular Refreshing:** Digital preservation will be an ongoing operation, requiring considerable recurring expense. Librarians may worry that they are committing their successors to operations for which there will be no funds. Considering the rapid increase in the storage capacities and the cost per byte decreasing, this may not become a problem. If a library can understand how it will fund the first refresh cycle in five to ten years, it can expect that the next refresh cycle will be so cheap as to be insignificant.

**Image V/S ASCI:** Some materials in digital libraries are available as images, and others as ASCII. In some cases these distinctions are inherent e.g. a photograph collection is always going to be images, and an OPAC is nearly always ASCII, In other cases, e.g. printed books and journals, both formats are possible. Image based products are provided usually by the publishers on CD-ROM, whereas community based products are in ASCII and available online. The widespread view is that online will generally win over CD-ROM and ASCII over image. Libraries, however, have to deal with both worlds.

Images occupy at least 10 times more space than ASCII. With the continuing fall in disc prices, the issue is not of storage cost, but that of network time and display capacity. For example, over a 64 Kbps ISDN line, a text page arrives in less than half a second while an image page takes 4 seconds, which is a definite lag. In practice therefore, image systems are limited to local networks (and CD-ROMs), while the ASCII is easily sent over the Web. Another problem is demand placed by images on local display. Most users still use *640x480* screens, not capable of displaying a whole page at once. Some providers due to reasons related to cost prefer the images. The cost *of* keying a book with 300 pages and *500,000* characters is about 50 times the cost *of* scanning. Other reasons being the simplicity *of* handling the illustrations or tables on the pages. We can expect that as OCR gets better, the image formats will disappear.

**Internetworking**

Another key issue is that of inter working of different digital libraries. Given the distribution of library resources around the world, no one expects that there would be a single digital re- source. This means that we need methods for finding either individual items or collections in different places, and assembling virtual collections that users can search or browse. All sorts of organizations are claiming the right to be the provider *of* information to the desktop:

online services, libraries, bookstores, publishers and telephone companies.

**Major Software Solutions**

There are about ten to fifteen major software packages for digital library development. Of this many are open source or free software. The remaining integrated puckages promoted by commercial organizations are not easily affordable even to our universities. We will discuss here the free software and libraries developed using them.

**DSpace**

DSpace is an open source software package that provides the tools for management of digital assets, and is commonly used as the basis for an institutional repository. It supports a wide variety of data, including books, theses, 3D digital scans of objects, photographs, film, video, research data sets and other forms of content. The data can be arranged as community collections of items, which bundle bit streams together.

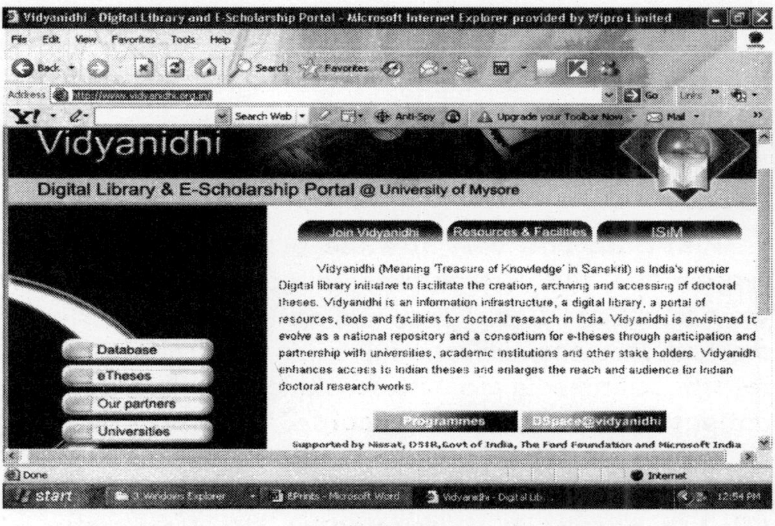


**Figure 1.2: Home page of Vidyanidhi Digital Archive**

DSpace is also intended as a platform for digital preservation activities. Since its release in 2002, as a product of the HP-MIT Alliance, it has been installed and is in use at about 300 institutions around the globe, from large universities to small colleges, cultural organizations, and research centers. It is shared under a BSD license, which enables users to customize or extend the software as needed.

DSpace is written in Java and JSP, using the Java Servlet API. It uses a relational database, and supports the use of PostgreSQL and Oracle. It makes its holdings available primarily via a web interface, but it also supports the Open Archives Initiative Protocol for Metadata Harvesting (OAI-PMH) and is capable of exporting METS (Metadata Encoding and Transmission Standard) packages. Future versions are likely to see increasing use of web services, and changes to the user interface layer.

The Mysore University project named Vidyanidhi, which is an online archive of dissertations published by Indian universities sponsored by the Union Science and Technology Ministry and supported by Ford Foundation and Microsoft is a good example of the Digital Library using DSpace from India. It can be accessed at http://www.vidyanidhi.org.in/

**EPrints**

EPrints is a very flexible platform for building repositories, and is recognized as the easiest and fastest way to set up digital archives and digital libraries of research literature, scientific data, student theses, project reports, multimedia artifacts, teaching materials, scholarly collections, digitized records, exhibitions and performances. EPrints is quick to install, easy to configure, and needs minimal maintenance. It is OAI-PMH Compliant. EPrints has been developed at the University of

Southampton School of Electronics and Computer Science and released under a GPL license.

EPrints is a Web and command-line application based on the LAMP architecture (but is written in Perl rather than PHP). It has been successfully run under Linux, Solaris and Mac OS X [2]. A version for Microsoft Windows is also available. EPrints is translated to languages other than English through (re distributable) language-specific XML phrase files. Existing translations include Bulgarian, French, German, Hungarian, Italian, Japanese, Russian, Spanish and Ukrainian. About 300 known archives are using EPrints worldwide.

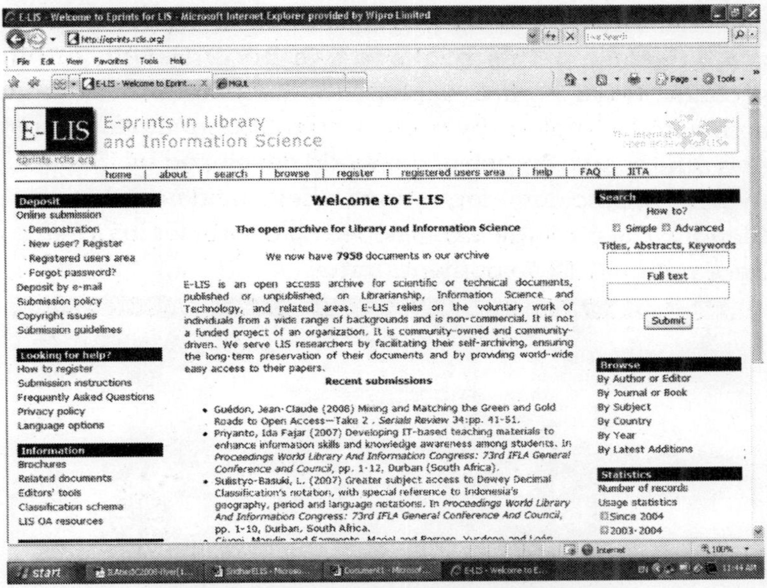


**Figure 1.3: Home page of E-LIS Archive in Library and Information Science**

E-LIS is the best example of digital library in the web running on EPrints. It is an international OA archive for scientific or technical documents, published or unpublished, on Librarianship, Information Science and Technology, and related areas. At present E-LIS is the biggest repository in Library and Information Science (LIS). E-LIS can be accessed at http://eprints.rclis.org/

**Nitya**

Nitya Archive, is a full text retrieval utility for the organization of records like books, old manuscripts, palm leaf manuscripts, paintings etc and information in digital libraries and CDROM publications. Searching of the Digital Library through its full text and opening of the required page of a book or leaf of a manuscript in it will be very fast. Nitya Archive uses high-level text compaction technique and sophisticated free text search and retrieval procedure. Any piece of information contained in any page of any document from the complete collections of Digital archives prepared using this package can be retrieved within seconds. Nitya Archive exploits the full potential of digital archiving technology by combining the capabilities of most powerful search engine in the world developed by UNESCO to achieve efficient information retrieval and is highly user-friendly. The package is developed by Center for Informatics Research and Development, India.

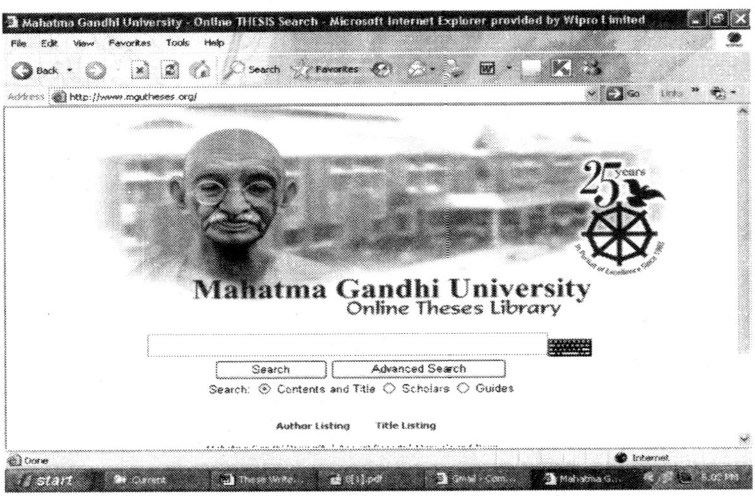


**Figure 1.4: Home Page of Mahatma Gandhi University Digital Library of Theses**

Beehive Digital Concepts, Cochin, has developed the Nitya dArch version for hosting digital libraries in the web. The package has multilingual search facility and satisfies UNICODE standards. Its metadata can be made OAI-PMH (Open Access initiative - Protocol for Metadata Harvest) compliant. It runs on Linux Server. It is built on PHP programming language in combination with MySQL. It has open database structure allowing future migration to OAI-PMH compliant packages. It is the only package presently available which can handle all Indian languages.

Most of the digital archives collections in local languages available in the web from India use Nitya Archive solutions. Mahatma Gandhi University (MGU) Online Theses Digital Library, which has been selected as one of the very best of the web resources for education and research by INTUTE, is a good example of digital libraries running on Nitya. The site can be accessed at http://www.mgutheses.org

### GenISIS

UNESCO, which has developed various, packages which can be used to develop digital libraries and archives, works to create an enabling environment, which is conducive to and facilitates universal access to information and knowledge. UNESCO also helps developing effective *info structures*, including developing information standards and management tools, strengthening libraries and archives key actors in knowledge societies, and fostering access at the community level. As part of this UNESCO has developed CDS/ISIS which is the most powerful package for database management in libraries. It is a generalized Information Storage and Retrieval system The Windows version WINISIS may run on a single computer or in a local area network. The JavaISIS client/server components allow remote database management over the Internet and are available for Windows and Linux.

UNESCO's GenISIS allows the user to produce HTML Web forms for CDS/ISIS database searching.

CDS/ISIS database management system and its related packages are the most significant contribution that made libraries the forerunners of ICT revolution. There had been a rapid growth of automated library systems all over the world after introduction of CDS/ISIS. The introduction of Windows version of the package WINISIS further extended its popularity and use. Now all over the world lakhs and lakhs of institutions use WINISIS for developing and managing digital libraries, GenISISWeb for , making them accessible with search mechanisms over Intranet/ Internet, and GenISISCD for publishing them with search engine in CDROMs.

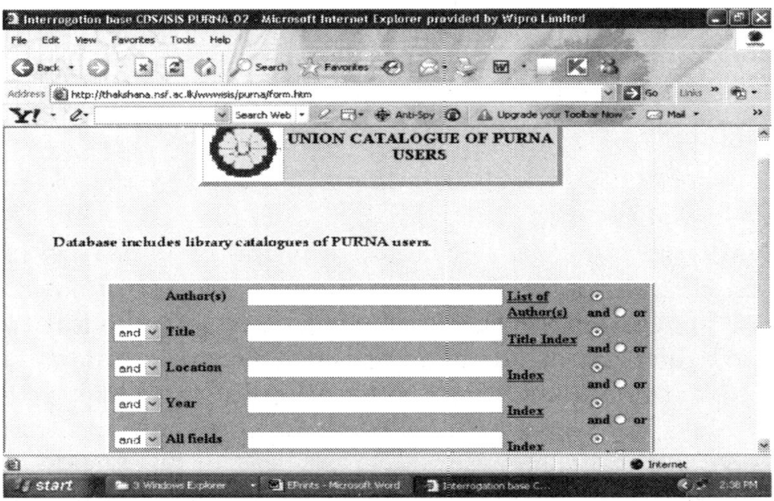


**Figure 1.5: Home Page of Archive of Sri Lanka Scientific & Technical Information Centre**

Various integrated information system like Nitya in India and PURNA in Sri. Lanka, which can handle digital libraries, were developed using CDS/ISIS. Of this PURNA uses the UNESCO packages in their pure form and is used by more than 85 libraries in Sri Lanka. Web module of PURNA was developed using GenISIS and it facilitates exploring the catalogue, loan records, serials register, reservation, viewing full text etc. The best example of a digital archive available in the web, which uses GenISIS, is the archives of Sri Lanka Scientific & Technical Information Centre under National Science Foundation. It can be accessed at http://thakshana.nsf.ac.lk/wwwisis/purna/form.htm. We will discuss UNESCO's packages in detail in the next Chapters.

**Future**

Digital libraries are expected to bring about significant improvements over current modes of information publishing and access methods. Educators, researchers and students across the world will be among the first to benefit from digital libraries, particularly those in developing countries.

# 2 HARDWARE & SOFTWARE

Digital Archive is an evolving area of research, development and application. Digital libraries archives are electronic information collections containing large and diverse repositories of digital objects, which can be accessed by a large number of geographically distributed users. *The can hold* text, images, maps, sounds, videos, different types of data sets as well as hyper textual multimedia compositions of such elements. This Chapter will cover the following aspects.

- Computer systems
- Scanners
- Power Supply
- Storage Media
- Scanning Software
- Application software
- e-book makes
- Optical Character Recognition

# HARDWARE & SOFTWARE

## HARDWARE AND SOFTWARE REQUIREMENTS

Digital library development requires computers and application software meant for different process related to digitization. There are highly advanced and powerful hardware and software for digital archiving/library purposes. They are meant to be used in huge collections having very brittle and complicated documents. But here we are limiting the requirements to very small collections. Very minimum systems are suggested.

For a small digitization project we will require a powerful computer, a scanner, an UPS and software for scanning, for preparing electronic documents, and a digital library software for organizing the collection in a retrievable way

### Computer Specification

Computer hardware and software are constantly changing. Latest machines available in the market will be fast enough to handle almost any scanning and other digitization tasks. Here are some minimum guidelines for computer hardware as per the technology and availability as on June 2009.

### Personal Computer

| | |
|---|---|
| Operating system installed | Windows Vista® Home Basic |
| Processor type | Intel® Pentium® Dual Core Processor E2200 |

| | |
|---|---|
| | 3.20 GHz, 1 MB Advanced Transfer Cache, 800 MHz System Bus |
| Cache | 1 MB Advanced Transfer Cache |
| Processor front side bus | 800 MHz System Bus |
| Chipset | nVidia nForce 630i |
| Memory type | DDR2-SDRAM |
| Standard memory | 1024MB |
| Memory slots | 2 DIMM |
| Internal drives | 320 GB |
| Hard disk drive speed | (7200 rpm) |
| Storage controller | Serial ATA hard drive |
| Optical drive type | SuperMulti SATA Drive |
| Optical drive speed | SuperMulti SATA Drive with Lightscribe Technology, Double Layer (8.5GB) 16x DVD±R, 8x DVD+RW, 6x DVD-RW, 8x DVD±R DL, 12x DVD-RAM, 16x DVD-ROM, 40x CDR, 32x CDRW, 40x CD-ROM (max speed) data transfer rates up to 6,000 KB/s (CD read/write) and 21,632 KB/s (DVD read/write) |
| Lightscribe | LightScribe |
| Graphic subsystem name | nVIDIA GeForce 7100 |
| Video RAM | TurboCache with 128MB dedicated graphics memory. Up to 319MB Total Available Graphics Memory as allocated by Windows Vista® |
| Internal audio | Integrated Intel High Definition Audio - 5.1 Surround Sound Ready |
| External I/O ports | 6 USB 2.0 ports (2 front, 4 rear), 2 |

| | |
|---|---|
| | PS/2, 1 FireWire® IEEE 1394 port, LAN |
| Expansion slots | 1 PCI Express (x16), 1 PCI Express (x1) |
| Memory card device | 15-in-1 Digital Media Reader |
| Network interface | Integrated 10/100 BaseT network interface (Broadband Ready) |
| Keyboard | HP low profile Multimedia Cordless keyboard (2.4GHz), HP Cordless, optical, 2-button scroller mouse |
| Monitor | 17 Inch LCD wide Screen Monitor |
| Softwares | Cyberlink Power2Go, CyberLink PowerDirector, Muvee autoProducer, Norton Internet Security 2008, Recovery CD Creator, Hard Drive based Application Recovery for reinstallation of applications and drivers, Hard Drive based System Recovery with option to keep user data files intact, PC Doctor, Preloaded Help & Support Center |

Workstations with specifications similar to that mentioned can be used for digital library development.

## Scanners

Flatbed scanners vary widely by model and manufacturer. Like computers, many basic scanners now have enough quality to do adequate scanning. We have to, look for a model from a major manufacturer and consider reviews published by computer magazines and websites before purchase. A large bed scanner (13 x 17 is a normal size) is desirable for digitizing large special collections materials.

The scanner we select should have the capability do quickly and efficiently all the scanning jobs that will come in an office in addition to scanning for digital library. It should have the facility to add automatic document feeder and scan at speeds up to 8 pages per minute and 4 images per minute. It should also have a transparent materials adapter to capture scans from 35 mm slides or negatives. Entry-level document management software should be available with the scanner. TWAIN drivers ensure compatibility with existing data management systems. The scanner should deliver high-quality scans at 2400 dpi optical resolution and 48-bit color. It should also have the features like fast preview scans, one-touch operation, and Imaging software for graphic arts and digital photography projects.

Detailed specification of two scanners from HP and UMAX are provided below. Scanners with similar specifications can be considered for small digital library development projects.

**HP Scan jet 5590 Digital Flatbed Scanner (L1910A)**

| | |
|---|---|
| Scan type | Flatbed, ADF |
| Optical scanning resolution | Up to 2400 dpi |
| Bit depth | 48-bit |
| Gray scale levels | 256 |
| Auto document feeder capacity | Standard, 50 sheets |
| Scan speed (ADF, A4) | up to 8 ppm; simplex mode, black and white, 200 dpi, 1-bit |
| Transparency adapter | Satellite; three slides or four 35 mm negative frames |
| Scan speed | 10 x 15 cm colour photo into Microsoft Word: less than 24 sec; OCR a full page of text into Microsoft Word: less than 36 sec; |

| | |
|---|---|
| | e-mail photo: less than 18 sec |
| Scan size maximum (flatbed) | 21.6 x 27.9 cm |
| Scan size maximum (ADF) | 210 x 356 mm (one-sided); 210 x 305 mm (two-sided) |
| Media types supported | Paper (banner, inkjet, photo, plain), envelopes, labels, cards (greeting, index), 3-D objects, 35-mm slides and negatives (using transparent materials adapter), iron-on transfers |
| Scan file format | Windows: BMP, JPEG, TIFF, TIFF compressed, PNG, PCX, Flashpix (FPX), PDF, PDF searchable, RTF, HTM, TXT; Macintosh: TIFF, PICT, JPEG, GIF, FlashPix, Plain Text, PDF, HTML, Rich Text |
| Scan speed in preview mode | 7 sec |
| Control panel | Scan, Copy, E-mail, Share-to-web, Save to PDF, Power Save, Cancel, Copy Colour/Black and White |
| Standard connectivity | Hi-Speed USB 2.0 |
| Compatible Operating Systems | Microsoft® Windows® 2000, XP Professional and Home Edition, certified for Windows Vista™; Mac OS X (10.1.5, 10.2 or higher) |

**UMAX Astra 7350 Specification**

The model is targeted at high-end users requiring scans of high quality and precision. This sturdily built scanner looks different when compared to most conventional scanners as its width and length are interchanged. It scans at a an optical resolution of 3200 x 6400 dpi at 48-bit color using the standard RGB color CCD sensor, with the maximum scan resolution being 19200 x 19200 dpi. Operating via the USB 2.0 interface, it scans a maximum area of 8.5"x11.7"(A4). 35 mm negatives can also be scanned using the additional black transparency cover provided. The scanner has one-touch buttons for most of the functions.

The software packages provided with the scanner includes Ulead Photo Express 4.0, FineReader 5.0 and Acrobat Reader 5.0.

The scanner is quick to warm up; it takes about mere 8 seconds. Users opine that text and images from newspapers scanned at the 72-150 dpi resolution gave good results with sharp color reproduction of black and white without any smudge or RGB grain presence. While the preview time is 12 seconds, the actual scan time comes to 22 seconds.

**Digital Cameras**

Most digital cameras are inadequate for reproduction of special collections materials. Digital camera set-ups that are adequate for reproducing archival materials, such as those made by PhaseOne or JenOptik, are very expensive and require substantial expertise to use. A cheap ordinary Digital Camera available in the local market can be acquired for using in the cases in which scanner cannot be used.

**Storage Media**

Currently the norm for storage is DVD (storage on CD and CD-RW media is not recommended). We should not use very cheap DVD media. We have to save our master images (and derivatives to be safe) onto DVD and make a 2nd copy for backup purposes. We have to store our media in jewel cases rather than envelopes, and label them for appropriate identification of their contents. When storing DVD media long term, the approximate lifespan before data loss occurs is approximately 5-10 years. For ideal preservation of digital materials, we should plan to recopy all of our DVD media after 5 years.

**Software Required**

In addition to the digital library software mentioned earlier Digital Library development will require various application software, like image editing software, word processing software, Optical character recognition software, scanning software etc in addition to the digital Library/Archive solution.

For most digital library applications Adobe Acrobat and for image processing applications in digital archiving Adobe Photoshop is the de facto standard and is recommended. Both are expensive than other packages used for the work, but the quality of documents and images produced by them have been shown to be greater than those produced by other software. Popular OCR software is Fine Reader and Omnipage. We will require all popular application software like word processors, etc. The main component in Digital Library development is Digital Library software about which we will discuss in detail in later chapters.

**Scanning Software**

Scanners also come with a driver application that operates the scanner and sends the image to application programmes. The features included in these applications are dependent on the scanner manufacturer, but they usually include the ability to preview, descreening functionality for halftone (dot-based) images, and color correction.

**Adobe Acrobat**

Adobe Acrobat software can be used to reliably share documents. It can create and distribute PDF files that preserve the formatting of the originals. It can also combine documents, images, spreadsheets, and web pages in a single PDF file, and quickly organize content or a document in a way in which it can communicate clearly and effectively. The documents made in Adobe can share information with virtually anyone in the world for using free Adobe Reader software which is used to open the Adobe documents is free.

Adobe acrobat can be used to control access to PDF files with document passwords and permissions. Set document permissions to define whether a file can be printed or changed. Apply passwords to help restrict document access. Digitally sign and certify documents to validate that they came from a trusted source. These are very important for digital libraries and archives.

**FineReader**

FineReader is an intelligent, professional level OCR software for creating editable and searchable files from scanned documents, PDF files and digital camera images. FineReader gives us the facility to unlock the data inside paper-based documents, images, and PDF files to substantially enhance our productivity and efficiency. It has Adaptive Document Recognition Technology (ADRT).

The programme has Superior recognition accuracy and layout retention. ADRT enables re-creation of document's logical structure and formatting. It has an intelligent Result-Driven Interface guiding the user to the best OCR result in fewer clicks. With automatic language detection and optimization for multi-core processor machines, performing any OCR task is quicker and easier in Fine Reader. It can recognize the languages of Chinese, Japanese, Thai and Hebrew. It has compatibility with Microsoft environment and Office Applications .

**OmniPage**

OmniPage is also a fastest and precise way to convert paper, PDF files, and digital camera pictures into files we can edit in our computer applications. It works with all scanners and we can capture text with a digital camera or iPhone. OmniPage lets us turn documents that would take hours to re-type into perfectly formatted documents in seconds. We can even turn scanned documents into specially formatted pages for easy reading. The developers claim that the improved OCR engines can deliver 99%+ accuracy for document conversion and archiving business critical documents. Converted documents look exactly like the original and are easier to edit, complete with columns, tables, bullets and graphics. Converting documents is easy. The Quick Convert View gets it done in seconds - there's no need to learn a lot of options and tools and any one with minimum computer awareness can use the package. In Digital library development we can turn PDF file into other application for easy editing. We can also transform documents into searchable versions of these formats and do full text indexing by digital library search utilities. Omnipage supports the widest range of output formats including PDF, HTML, Corel® WordPerfect®, Microsoft® Word, Excel® and PowerPoint® 2007 plus many more formats. It recognizes over 120 languages and can be used to process, edit and store documents in those languages from anywhere in the world.

# 3

# UNESCO SOFTWARE

UNESCO works to create an enabling environment, which is conducive to and facilitate universal access to information and knowledge. UNESCO helps developing effective 'infostructures', including developing information standards and management tools, strengthening libraries and archives as key actors in knowledge societies, and fostering access at the community level. UNESCO, has developed various, packages which can be used to develop digital libraries and archives. This Chapter will discuss UNESCO's activities in the ICT related areas and will introduce the packages developed by it.

Educational Priorities:
Natural Sciences
Social and Human Sciences
Culture
Communication and Information
Community Networks
Information Processing Tools
CDS/ISIS, WINISIS, GENISIS,
IDAMS, Greenstone

# UNESCO SOFTWARE

## UNESCO SOFTWARE FOR DIGITAL LIBARIES

United Nations Educational, Scientific and Cultural Organization (UNESCO) is a specialized agency of the United Nations. It was founded in the year 1945. Its main objective was to use Education, Social and Natural Science, Culture and Communication as the means to build peace in the minds of men.

The commitment of UNESCO to the crucial issue of the free flow of information and access to knowledge sources is very much inspired by its Constitution, which states that "the wide diffusion of culture, and the education of humanity for justice and liberty and peace are indispensable to the dignity of man and constitute a sacred duty which all the nations must fulfill in a spirit of mutual assistance and concern".

UNESCO functions as a laboratory of ideas and a standard-setter to forge universal agreements on emerging ethical issues. It serves as a clearinghouse for the dissemination and sharing of information and knowledge. It helps Member States to build their human and institutional capacities in diverse fields, promotes international co-operation among them in the fields of education, science, culture and communication. Since its inception UNESCO is working to create the conditions for genuine dialogue based upon respect for shared values and the dignity of each civilization and culture.

This role is critical, particularly in the face of terrorism, which constitutes an attack against humanity. The world urgently requires global visions of sustainable development based upon observance of human rights, mutual respect and the alleviation of poverty, all of which lie at the heart of UNESCO's mission and activities. Through its strategies and activities, UNESCO is actively pursuing the Millennium Development

The goals, UNESCO strives to achieve by 2015 is especially those aiming to reducing by half the proportion of people living in extreme poverty in developing countries, achieving universal primary education in all countries, eliminating gender disparity in primary and secondary education, helping countries to implement a national strategy for sustainable development, and reversing current trends in the loss of environmental resources.

The Preamble to the Constitution of UNESCO declares that 'since wars begin in the minds of men, it is in the minds of men that the defenses of peace must be constructed'.

In order that a unanimous, lasting and genuine peace may be secured, the Preamble declares that the States which are party to the Constitution believed 'in full and equal opportunities for education for all, in the unrestricted pursuit of objective truth and in the free exchange of ideas and knowledge".

As defined by the Constitution, the purpose of UNESCO is: "to contribute to peace and security by promoting collaboration among nations through education, science and culture in order to further universal respect for justice, for the rule of law and for the human rights and fundamental freedoms which are affirmed for the peoples of the world, without distinction of race, sex, language or religion, by the Charter of the United Nations'.

UNESCO deploys its action in the fields of Education,

Natural Sciences, Social and Human Sciences, Culture, Communication and Information to achieve the above-mentioned objectives.

UNESCO has from 1945 worked to improve education worldwide through technical advice, standard setting, innovative projects, capacity building and networking.

**UNESCO's Educational Priorities:**

UNESCO's Educational Priorities are: basic education for all, with special attention being given to literacy, HIV/AIDS prevention education and teacher training; secondary education, including technical and vocational education and training as well as science and technology education; promoting quality education, with special reference to values education and teacher training and higher education.

**Natural Sciences**

UNESCO has developed several international programmes to better assess and manage the Earth's resources. The Organization also helps reinforce the capacities of developing countries in the sciences, engineering and technology. UNESCO's priorities in the field of Natural Sciences are: water and associated eco-systems; oceans; capacity-building in the basic and engineering sciences, the formulation of science policies and the promotion of a culture of maintenance; promoting the application of science, engineering and appropriate technologies for sustainable development, natural resource use and management, disaster preparedness and alleviation and renewable sources of energy.

**Social and Human Sciences**

The social and human sciences have a vital role to play in helping to understand and interpret the social, cultural and economic environment. They provide research, identify and analyze trends, and propose paths of action.

UNESCO's priorities in the field of Social and Human Sciences covers: ethics of science and technology, with emphasis on bioethics; promotion of human rights and the fight against all forms of discrimination, racism, xenophobia and related intolerance through activities; foresight, philosophy, human sciences, democracy and the enhancement of human security; and management of social transformation

**Culture**

According to UNESCO preserving and respecting the specificity of each culture, while ensuring that it preserves and respects the specificities of another culture, and involving it in an approach that bring them together and extends beyond them in a more interactive and interdependent world, is the challenge which must be met by the international community and, on its behalf, by UNESCO and its partners. UNESCO's cultural priorities cover: promoting cultural diversity, with special emphasis on the tangible and intangible heritage; cultural policies as well as intercultural and interfaith dialogue and understanding; cultural industries and artistic expressions.

**Communication and Information**

Communication and Information programmes are rooted in UNESCO's Constitution, which requires the Organization to promote the "free flow of ideas by word and image". The main objective for UNESCO is to build a knowledge society based on the sharing of knowledge and incorporating all the socio-cultural and ethical dimensions of sustainable development. UNESCO's priorities in the field of Communication and Information are: empowering people through access to information and knowledge with special emphasis on freedom of expression; promoting communication development; advancing the use of ICTs for education, science and culture

The Communication and Information Sector (CI) was established in its present form in 1990. The Communication and Information Sector consists of: the Communication Development Division, the Division for Freedom of Expression, Democracy and Peace, and the Information Society Division. Two intergovernmental programmes: the International Programme for the Development of Communication (IPDC) and the Information for All Programme (IFAP) works under the sector. The principal strategic objectives of the Sector's programmes are: promoting the free flow of ideas and universal access to information, promoting the expression of pluralism and cultural diversity in the media and world information networks, promoting access for all to ICTs

**Community Networks**

The development of networks ensures equitable access to services and contents especially in the public domain as well as facilitating the free flow of information. In promoting the development of electronic networks, UNESCO lays emphasis on policies and strategies to develop the most appropriate methodology to meet the specific needs of the different communities. Through its global and regional networks, the Organization seeks to effectuate social development, democratization and good governance. By providing access to relevant information in an interactive format and in an easily assimilated form, UNESCO fosters capacities to acquire new knowledge and skills.

Regional information networks, virtual laboratories and learning communities and other information networks offer a new paradigm for global cooperation using traditional and multimedia technologies to promote applications in the Organization's fields of competence.

Archives and libraries are essential components of any strategy aimed at improving information access, both for the public at large and for specialized groups. Since its creation, UNESCO has contributed to the reinforcement of these types of services.

The development of information technologies, and in particular the Internet, has created a completely new environment in which the role of traditional information services must be thoroughly revised. The potential of networking, cooperation and digitization modify substantially the functions of acquiring, storing and disseminating information and knowledge. Here, special attention must be paid to the least developed countries so that they do not lag behind technological advances.

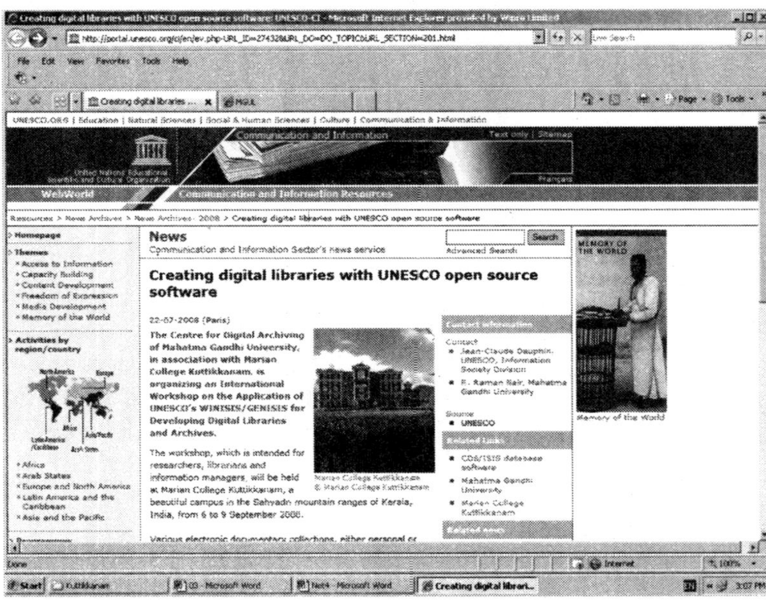


**Figure 3.1: UNESCO's Announcement on the GenISIS Workshop at Kuttikkanam, India**

In the area of archives, UNESCO, through its Records and Archives Management Programme - RAMP (established in 1979) aims at:

- Making the general public and decision-makers aware of the importance of records and archives for planning and development as well as safeguarding of the national heritage;
- Assisting Member States in the establishment of efficient records and archives management infrastructures through standardization, archival legislation, training, and enhancing infrastructure (buildings and equipment);
- Promoting international debates on main issues in the archival field
- Promoting E-Governance to enable the public sector's use of information and communication technologies with the aim of improving information and service delivery, encouraging citizen participation in the decision-making process and making government more accountable, transparent and effective.

The major on-going UNESCO activity in the field of e-governance is a crosscutting project on E-Governance Capacity-Building. This project aims at promoting the use of ICT tools in municipalities to enhance good governance through the development of training modules for local decision-makers in Africa and Latin America.

The "Global survey on on-line governance" and the "Country profiles of e-governance" were undertaken by UNESCO in cooperation with the Commonwealth Network of Information Technology for Development Foundation (COMNET-IT).

**Information Processing Tools**

In the digital age, software is essential for knowledge management and sharing. UNESCO has therefore accumulated significant experience in facilitating the development of some key software tools for processing information. These software tools are distributed free-of-charge and the objective is to empower the users by giving them access to some key technology for development and knowledge sharing, that most of them otherwise could not afford. The development model is based upon international cooperation and the software tools are continuously enriched, modified and updated with the co-operation of a community of experts from different countries. UNESCO develops, maintains and disseminates, free-of-charge, interrelated software packages for database management (CDS/ISIS) and data mining/statistical analysis (IDAMS) as well as for archives management.

CDS/ISIS developed by provides facilities for storing documents electronically and for advanced information retrieval. CDS/ISIS is used worldwide for managing databases in libraries and information centers. Greenstone is a suite of software for building and publishing digital library collections. It provides a new innovative way of organizing and publishing information on the Internet or on CD-ROM. IDAMS is a software for numerical information processing, i.e. data management, data mining and statistical analysis. The UNESCO Free Software Portal gives access to documents and websites, which are references for the Free Software/Open Source Technology movements. UNESCO Free software shown in Figure 3.2 portal can be reached at : http://portal.unesco.org/ci/en/ev.php-URL_ID= 1542&URL_ DO= DO_TOPIC&URL_SECTION =201.html

**CDS/ISIS**

CDS/ISIS is a generalized Information Storage and Retrieval system. The Windows version may run on a single computer or in a local area network. The JavaISIS client/ server components allow remote database management over the Internet and are available for Windows, Linux and Macintosh. Furthermore, GenISIS allows the user to produce HTML Web forms for CDS/ISIS database searching. The ISIS_DLL provides an API for developing CDS/ISIS based applications.

Micro CDS/ISIS is an advanced non-numerical information storage and retrieval software developed by UNESCO since 1985 to satisfy the need expressed by many institutions, especially in developing countries, to be able to streamline their information processing activities by using modern (and relatively inexpensive) technologies.

The software was originally based on the Mainframe version of CDS/ISIS, started in the late '60s, thus taking advantage of several years of experience acquired in database management software development. Several partners contributed to its development through the years.

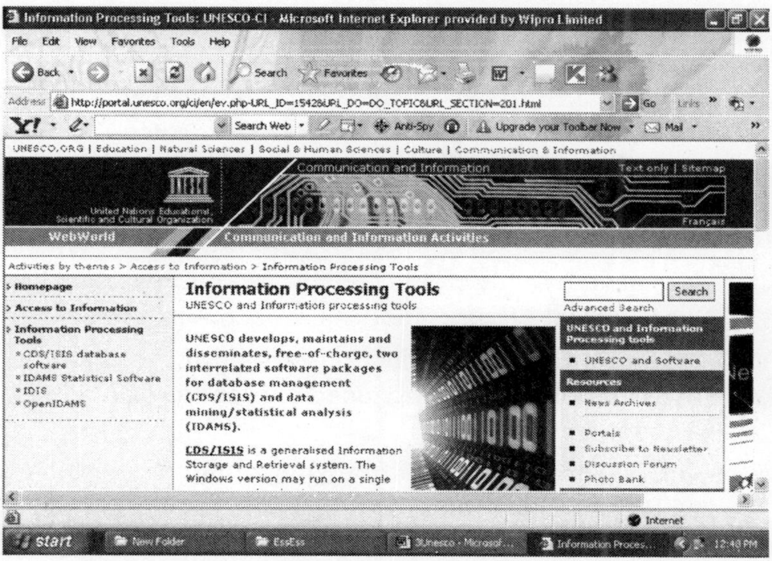


**Figure 3.2: UNESCO Site for Downloading Free Software and Manuals**

## CDS/ISIS for Windows

The development of the Windows version was the result of strategic development policy decision aiming at maintaining the leading role CDS/ISIS has played and is still playing on the international scene.

The following are the major features of the CDS/ISIS software:

- the handling of variable length records, fields and sub fields, thus saving disk space and making it possible to store greater amounts of information;
- the handling of repeatable fields;
- a data base definition component allowing the user to define the data to be processed for a particular application;
- a data entry component for entering and modifying data through user-created data base specific worksheets;
- an information retrieval component using a powerful search language providing for field-level and proximity search operators, in addition to the traditional and/or/not operators, as well as free-text searching;
- a powerful sort and report generation facility allowing the user to easily create any desired printed products, such as catalogues, indexes, directories, etc.;
- a data interchange function based on the ISO 2709 international standard used by leading data base producers;
- an integrated application programming language (CDS/ISIS Pascal and the ISIS_DLL), allowing the user to tailor the software to specific needs;
- functions allowing the user to build relational data bases, though CDS/ISIS is not based over a relational model;

- powerful hypertext functions allow to design complex user interfaces.

A Windows interface between CDS/ISIS and IDAMS, the UNESCO software for statistical analysis, has also been developed. From the outset, CDS/ISIS was created as a multi-lingual software, providing integrated facilities for the development of local linguistic versions. Thus, although UNESCO distributes only the English, French and Spanish versions of the package, user-developed versions exist in virtually all languages, including special versions which UNESCO helped in developing, for Arabic, Chinese and Korean. Versions for a few Indian languages also have been developed.

**DOS and Windows Compatibility**

No conversion is needed when moving from CDS/ISIS DOS to CDS/ISIS for Windows. However, formatting language functions are just 95% compatible. In some cases we may find some syntax errors appearing: we may have to adapt our display format to the new one. In terms of search engine, the two versions are totally compatible: both can use the same I/F (inverted file). The data entry worksheet are also compatible but the screens will appear different. CDS/ISIS for Windows (WiINISIS) is fully compatible with all Windows Operating Systems.

**User Manuals and Documentation**

A number of manuals are available for this software, including the official reference manual, recently updated and the CDS/ISIS Handbook. Other manuals contributed by independent authors are also available in UNESCO site for downloading and are listed at the end of this volume under the heading References and Further Reading.

**GenISIS**

GENISIS is an authoring software (for Win32) for

visually producing web forms to query CDS/ISIS databases. There are two versions of the tool: GenisisWeb, for web publishing and GenisisCD for developing CDROM interfaces for CDS/ISIS databases. GenISIS was originally developed by the former IBISCUS Association (France) for UNESCO and it is now available free of charge on the UNESCO FTP site. The software is written in Microsoft Visual Basic. Its source code is also freely available. GenISIS is programmed by Pierre Chabert. Available interface languages are English and French. Additional language translations can be developed by users. GenISIS, basically implements the following steps:

- the web query form (with field selection and index access);
- the display of query results;
- the display of a particular record's details;
- test the application;

For GenisisWeb, testing the generated application will require the use of a local web server. Finally, depending on which version of GENISIS you are using, it is possible to export the generated application to a real internet/intranet server (Windows, Unix, Linux) or to prepare the structure of the CDROM for the copy. GENISIS is based on the Web CDS/ISIS interface WWWISIS by BIREME.

**IDAMS**

IDAMS is a software package for processing and analyzing numerical data. It provides a great number of data manipulation and validation facilities and a wide range of classical and advanced statistical techniques. Interactive components allow for construction of multidimensional tables, graphical exploration of data and time series analysis. WinIDAMS software (IDAMS for 32-bit Windows operating system) as well as its documentation are available in English, French, Portuguese and Spanish. IDIS is a tool for direct data exchange between CDS/ISIS and IDAMS.

Knowledge and training in the use of information processing tools is as important as the tools themselves. At present, UNESCO offers various forms of traditional training in the use of CDS/ISIS and IDAMS. A computerized tutorial "How to work with WinIDAMS", available both on stand-alone PC configurations and in virtual courses through the Internet is available in English, French, Portuguese and Spanish.

**Greenstone**

Greenstone is a suite of software for building and distributing digital library collections. It provides a new way of organizing information and publishing it on the Internet or on CD-ROM. Greenstone is produced by the New Zealand Digital Library Project at the University of Waikato, and developed and distributed in cooperation with UNESCO and the Human Info NGO. It is open-source, multilingual software, issued under the terms of the GNU General Public License.

The aim of the Greenstone software is to empower users, particularly in universities, libraries, and other public service institutions, to build their own digital libraries. Digital libraries are radically reforming how information is disseminated and acquired in UNESCO's partner communities and institutions in the fields of education, science and culture around the world, and particularly in developing countries. This software can encourage the effective deployment of digital libraries to share information and place it in the public domain.

# 4 DIGITIZATION

Conversion of pages of books, images or other documents into required digital formats as well as transforming from different digital formats to an uniform format for incorporation in the digital library forms the preliminary work in digital library development. This chapter mainly will introduce converting paper document collections to digital format as well as creating and organizing electronic books from printed books and computer readable texts as well as using Scanning Software, Adobe Acrobat, and Optical Character Recognition programmes

# DIGITIZATION

## CONVERTING TO DIGITAL FORM

### Digitization Process

Most of the Scanners have a manual or product tour included in their software program. We can print this manual which will generally be in .pdf format using the **Print** command on the **File** menu. Or we can use the product tour, which is a fast and easy way to explore the capabilities of the scanner and see some interesting ways in which we can use the scanner to meet our needs. Mostly the product tour will be in Scanner's **Help** menu. We have to go to the Scanner program from Start Menu then go to Help Menu and then click Product Tour if it is available.

We can start scanning from one of these places:

- the scanner buttons
- the Scan Software provided with the scanner that is installed in the computer
- the programme for the format into which the scanned document is to be converted like MS Word, Adobe Acrobat, Adobe Photoshop, Paint etc.

Where we start depends on what we want to do with the scan and on our own preferences. In book digitization work it is better do the work from inside the concerned programme like Adobe Acrobat

We can use the scanner buttons, which are shortcuts, when we want to start at the scanner, scan quickly without making changes and want to scan an item using the default settings optimized for the destination we choose.

We can use the Scanner Software when want to view or change in resolution, or we want to do cropping, or resizing a scanned image before we incorporate that into the collection or send it. Also when we want to send the scanned image or file to a destination, and there is no button on the scanner for that destination the Scanner software can be used.

We can start scanning from within another program when we want to bring a scanned item into an open program, such as our word-processing program, or image processing program or e-book creation program like Adobe Acrobat.

The program in which we are working need to be compliant with scanner software. A program is compliant if a command like **Acquire Image** or **From Scanner** appears on a menu such as the **File** menu.

We can start scanning from the Scanner Software when we want to make copies and need to make standard copy adjustments, such as reducing or enlarging or lightening or darkening.

To start the Scanner Software we have to Click **Start** menu, then point to **Programs**, and then point to the name of Scanner Software that will be available under its.

Before placing items in the scanner, adhere to the following guidelines for selecting and preparing them to prevent damage to the items and the scanner.

The scanner glass can scan the widest range of items up to its size , including: all paper items, news clippings, old or worn photographs or documents, printed books, items containing tears, perforations, punch holes, wrinkles, or curls, flatter, three-dimensional items such as pages in books, fabric, and paper with texture. We have to avoid placing items with sharp edges in the scanner. Doing so can damage the scanner. Before placing an item on the scanner glass, we have to make sure the item is free of wet glue, correction fluid, or other contaminating substances.

Some scanners have transparency adapter also which can be used to scan photographic negatives, 35 mm slides, and other transparent media.

**Book Scanning**

Doing our first scan is easy. This section describes how to scan a book for inclusion in digital document collection using the scanning software. Before scanning, we have to load the item in the scanner.

We have to choose an item to scan, such as a printed page or a book. Then we have to place the item face down on the scanner glass as in Figure 4.1: and close the lid.

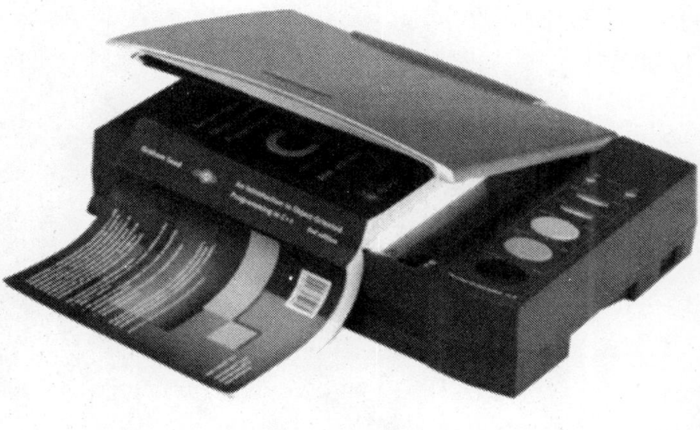

**Figure 4.1: Loading the Book in Scanner**

Scanning software supplied with most of the scanners provides preview capabilities and tools for changing an image. Some of the changes we can make include:

- select only part of, or crop, the preview image to become the final scanned image,

- change the resolution, resize the scanned image and also to change the contrast

In procedures discussed below the Scanner software used is HP PrecisionScan Pro. The interface of most of the Scanner software will have similar menus and options. The only thing is the lay out of the front-end window will be different.

On the **Start** menu, point to **Programs**, and click scanning software by the name of the software (eg: **HP PrecisionScan Pro)**. The software starts as in Figure 4.2.

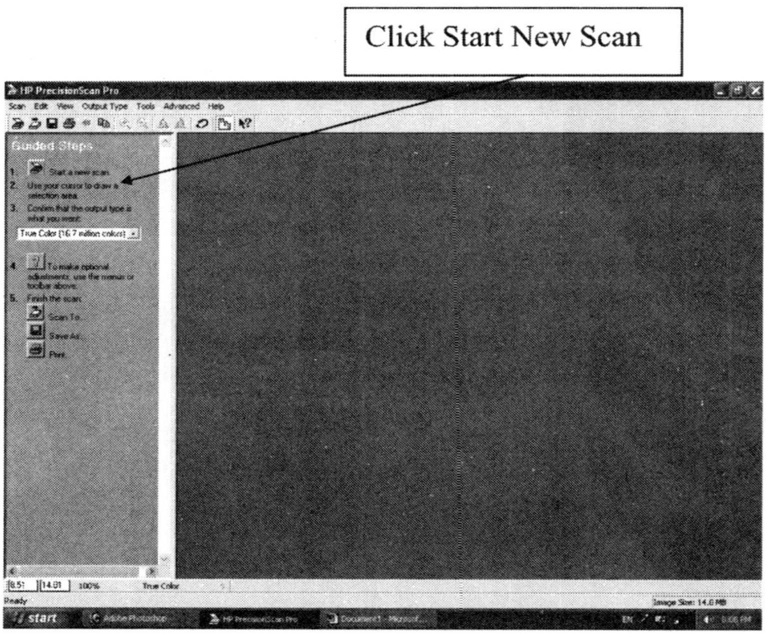


**Figure 4. 2: Scanning Programme**

In Scan menu if the Guided Steps are available/ visible, click **Scan** or **New Scan** or **Start New Scan** as available..

The scanned image appears in the Computer screen inside scanning software window as in Figure 4.3.

This scanned image is the preview image. We can make changes such as selecting only part of the image or adjusting the contrast. When we send the image to another program, or save it as a file, the scanner performs a final scan of the item that includes any changes we made. Directions for making optional adjustments and completing the scan are provided below.

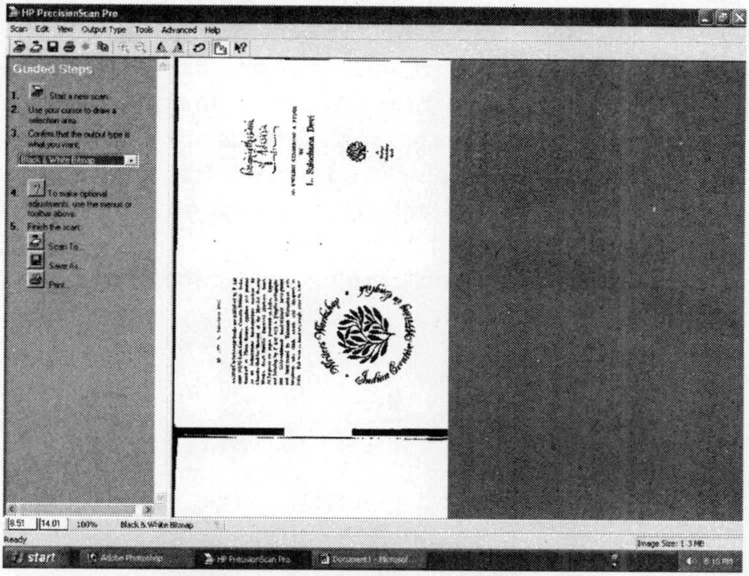


**Figure 4.3: Scanned Image Appears**

## Selecting the area to be scanned

Once a scanned image appears in the Scan Software, we have to select the area that should come in the final scanned image by creating a selection area. For this we have to move the cursor over the area we want and click on one corner of the area we select and drag the cursor to the opposite corner to draw a rectangular selection area. When we create a selection area, a dotted selection border appears around the area as in the Figure 4.4 If we click under **Edit** menu, in **Select All** option the entire scanner bed, including blank areas, will get selected. We can click on a handle of the selection border and drag to resize.

**Selecting the Output Type**

We can change the output type our self when we want. We have to choose the output type based on how we will use the final scanned image as well as the type of item we are scanning. The output types will be normally given in the Menu and here it is provided in the left side panel of the Scan Software programme. For book digitization **Black and White Bitmap** is the accepted type. For black and white photographs **Gray scale** can be used. For color images **True color** can be used. **Here the sample being a book we can select** Black and White Bitmap **as in the Figure 4.5.**

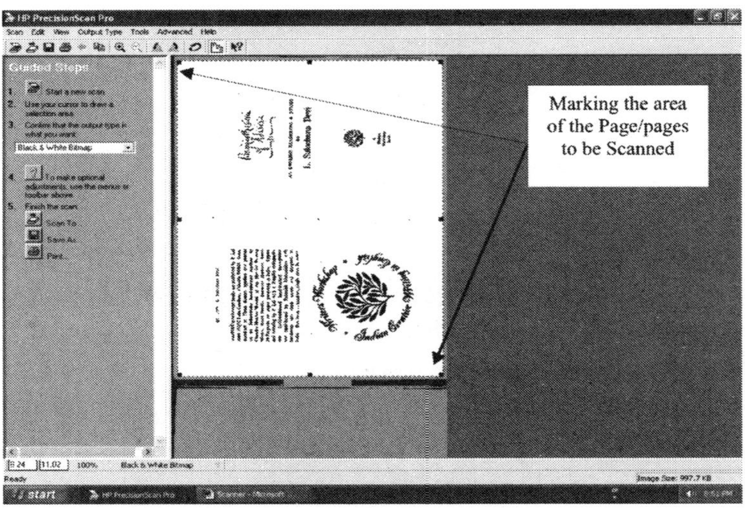


**Figure 4.4: Area Selected for Scanning**

Then most scanning software will have provisions for making various adjustments. This can be done or defaults can be accepted. Then we have to decide to what program the scanner should send the scanned copy of the document. Here the sample being a book from which e-version/book is to be generated for inclusion in digital library **Adobe Acrobat** is the accepted standard program for creating pdf. We have to select scan to and then Adobe Acrobat as shown in the Figure 4.6.

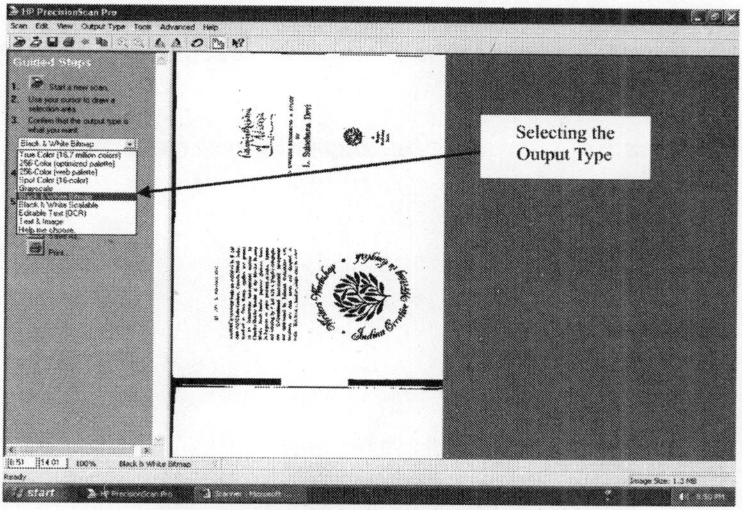


**Figure 4.5: Selecting the Output Type**

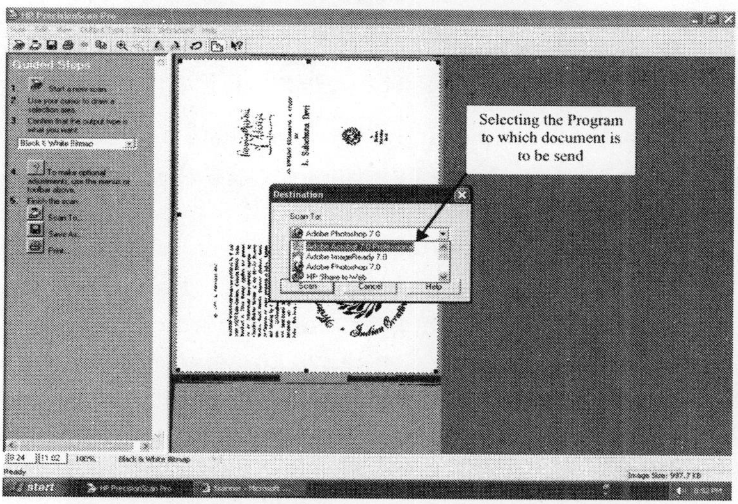


**Figure 4.6: Selecting the Program to which Scanned Document is to be Send**

Again we have to Click the Scan Button, which will enable the scanner to scan the area selected by us into the selected program to which we asked the computer to send the scanned file. The Scanned pages will be send to Adobe Acrobat and the Acrobat Programme will automatically open with the scanned page of the book as in the following figure.

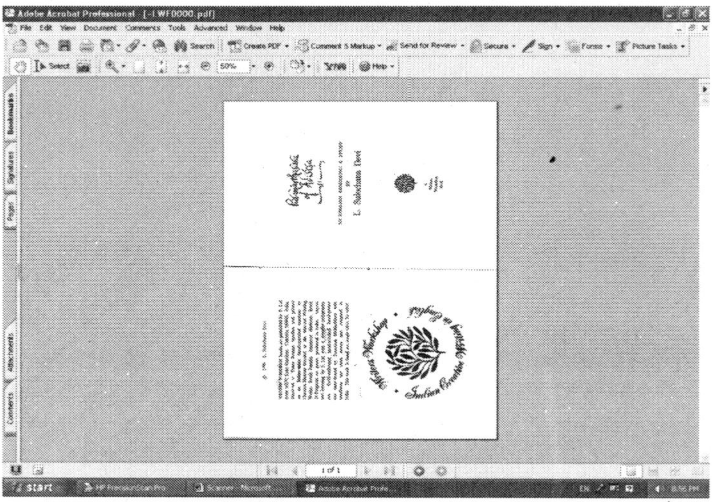


**Figure 4.7: Scanned Pages Opens in Adobe Acrobat**

Then we can give File name. Give Save Option to save the File and File name can be provided as Paramarthasara the name of the book or under any mnemonic name.

In the same way photograph or other images can be scanned. While scanning we have to select the areas of the scanner bed/photograph to be scanned and True color as output type if it is a color photograph or picture as in as in Figure 4.8.

In **Scan to** option we have to select **Adobe Photoshop** or other programmes and we can save the photograph in the required format in the concerned programme.

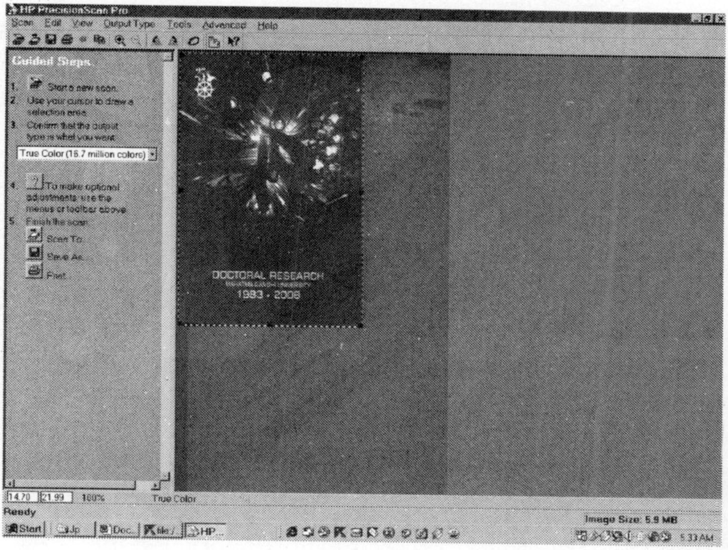


**Figure 4.8: Digitizing Color Photograph**

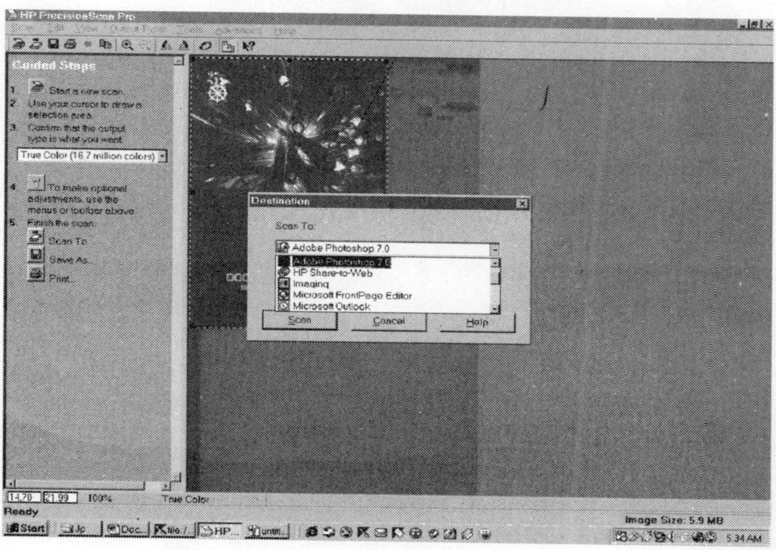


**Figure 4.9: Selecting Adobe Photoshop**

## Scanning From a Programme

We can also scan the pages of a book or an image from an application programme like Adobe Acrobat, Adobe Photoshop, Paint or Microsoft Word. For book Digitization it is always advisable to work from inside the Adobe Acrobat. For this first we have Open Adobe Acrobat.

To open Adobe Acrobat from Start Menu we have to Select **Programme**, and under it **Adobe Acrobat**.

Now Adobe Acrobat will Open. In Adobe Acrobat we have to Select **Create PDF** and under it the Option **From the Scanner** as in the following figure.

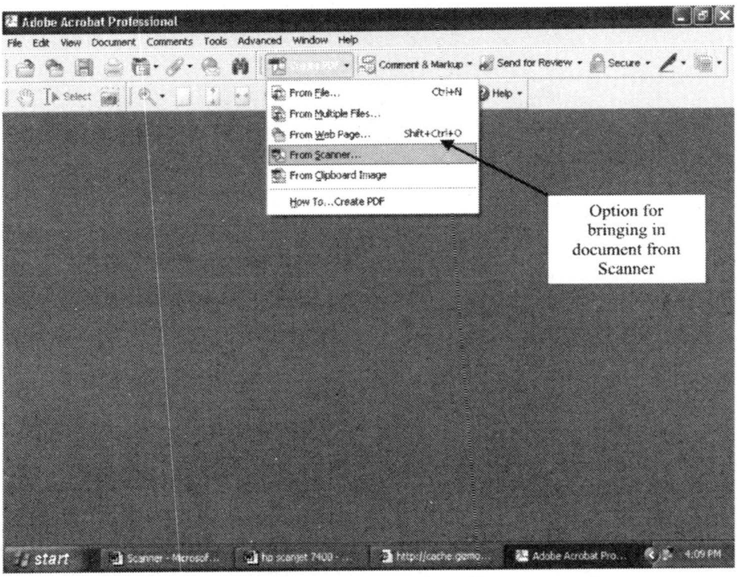


**Figure 4.10: Selecting Importing Document from Scanner Inside Adobe Acrobat**

If we have already loaded the book in the scanner Adobe will automatically open the Scanner program, scan the pages and bring the pages to Scan Programme and we will get the screen as in Figure 4.3. then we have to finish the processes explained in Figures 4.3 to 4.7. Then after accepting the finalized pages as in Figure 4.7 Adobe Acrobat will ask if the next page also is to be digitized. If we upload the new page in the scanner and say YES the next page also will be scanned. But we have to make the settings for each and every page. The same process can be repeated or short cuts explained below can be used to continue the work.

At any time we can save the work and close the programme. Again we can reopen a saved file and continue the work. So work can also be started from an existing file, which may contain the part of the book already digitized.

To start the work from an existing file or to continue the work from an earlier file in which a few pages of the book have already been digitized we have to

Go to **Start Menu** and select **Programme**, and under it **Adobe Acrobat**.

Now Adobe Acrobat will Open. In Adobe Acrobat from **File** menu we have to Open the earlier file **Paramarthasara** (we have saved by selecting **Open** and then **My Documents** where we have saved the file and then **Paramarthasara**) The pdf file **Paramarthasara** will open with the pages we have already digitized. We have to Select **Create PDF** and under it the Option **From the Scanner** as in the Figure 4.11.

While scanning the pages we can save the settings we used for the first page or other page which will avoid some repetitive jobs and help to speed up the work.

Once we have marked the area to be scanned and output type and the programme to which the file is to be send to etc we can save the settings that we so defined. For that as shown in the Figure 4.12 we have to select **Scan**, then **Settings**, and then **Save.**

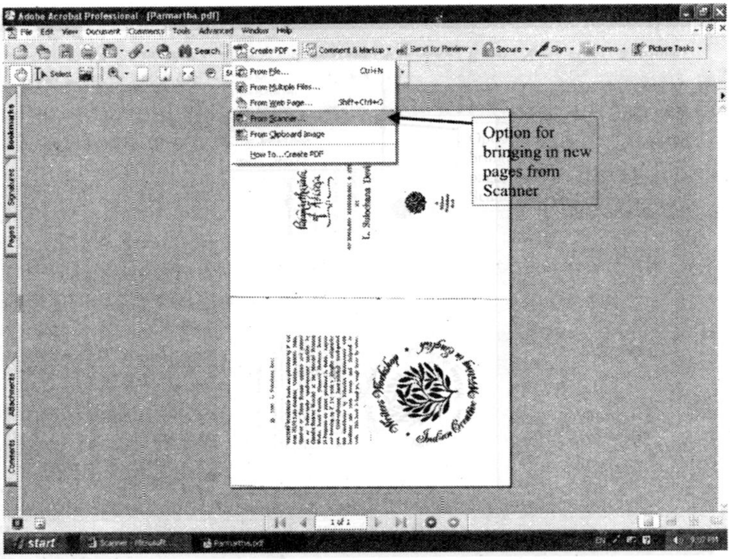


**Figure 4. 11 : Scanning Pages into an Existing File with Pages Scanned Earlier**

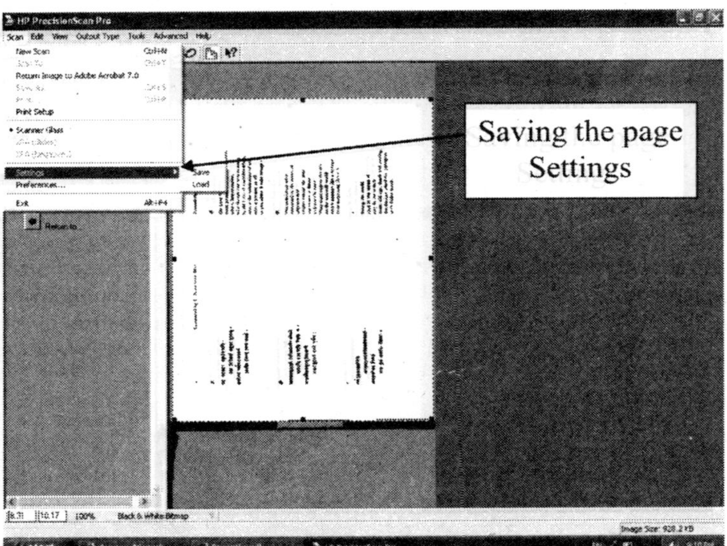


**Figure 4.12: Saving the Page Settings for Future Scans**

Then a window as in Figure 13 will come to the screen. In that we have to specify the file name under which the settings is to be saved. We can give **Paramarthasara**; the name of the book or a similar name.

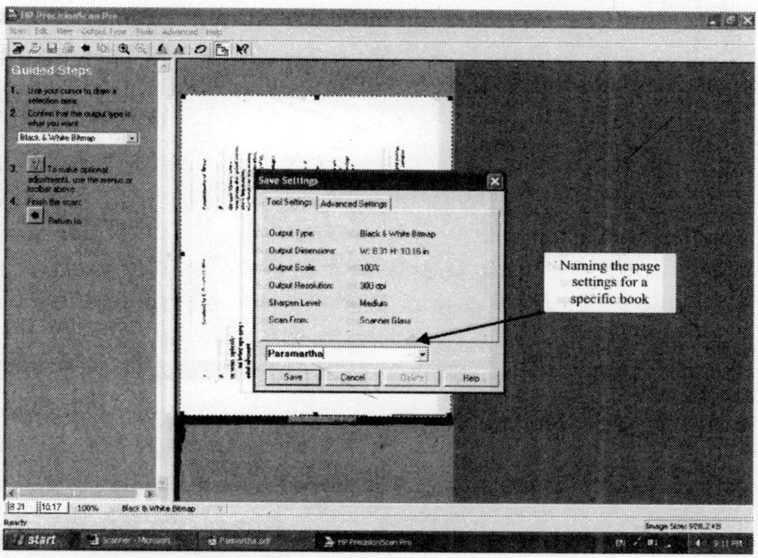


**Figure 4.13: Saving the Page Settings**

After the current page is sent to Adobe Acrobat as done earlier the Adobe Acrobat will ask as in the Figure 4.14 if the Next page is to be scanned or not. We have to give the option NEXT.

Then the next page will be scanned and brought to the programme. Then from the scanner programme we have to select the **Scan** Option and its sub option **Load** as in Figure 4.15.

Then the screen as in Figure 4.16 will come and from that we have to select the settings we have saved in the name Paramarthasara. This process can be repeated for all pages. If any page required any special change in the settings, for that page that changes can be made.

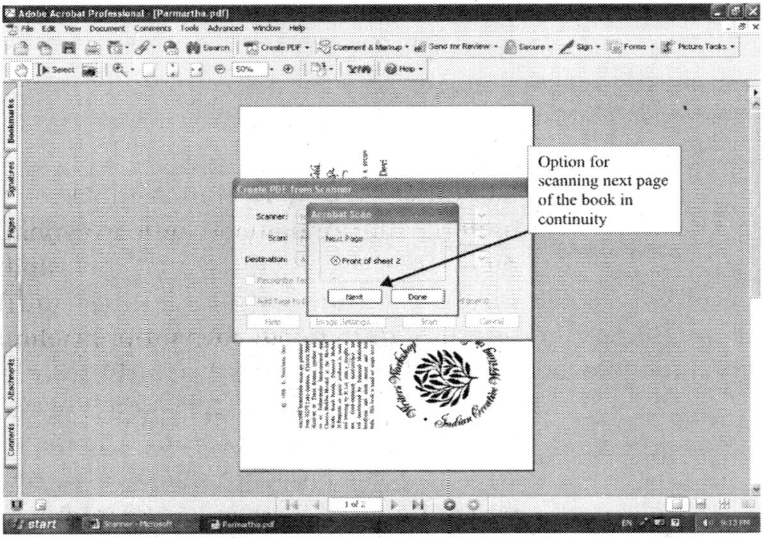


**Figure 4.14: Option for Scanning the Pages in a Sequence**

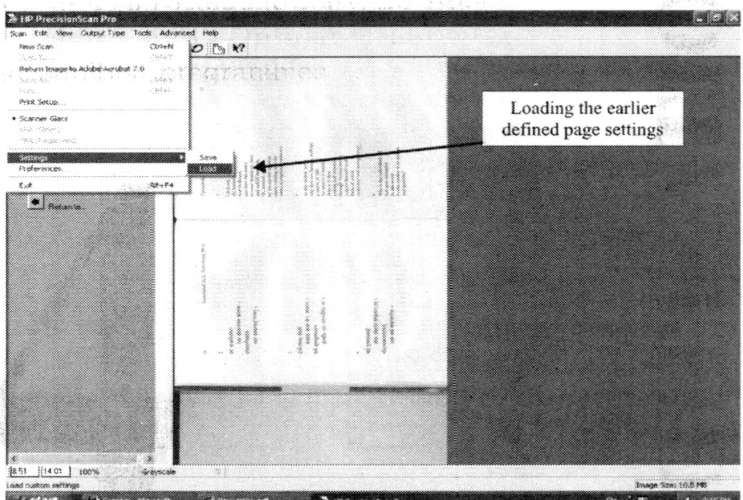


**Figure 4.15: Loading Predefined Page Settings**

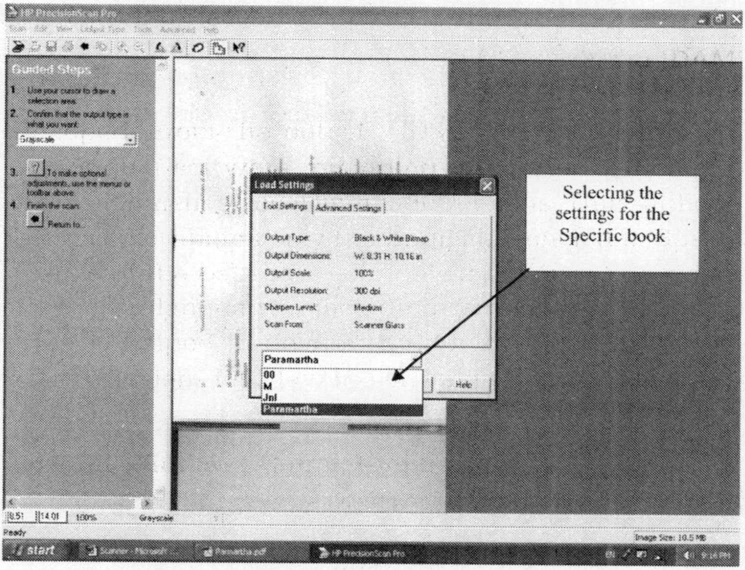


**Figure 4.16: Choosing the Required Settings from Predefined items**

## Rotating the Pages

For convenience in book scanning and to get two pages scanned at the same time we place the book pages sideways.

We can rotate the image or pdf page in 90-degree increments clockwise or counterclockwise. We might need to rotate the image of pages if we placed the bottom of the item at the top of the scanner glass, or if the item was sideways.

To rotate the pages of a book clockwise in Adobe Acrobat we have to select the option from the **Tools** menu, Document and sub option under it Rotate the pages as in Figure 4.17.

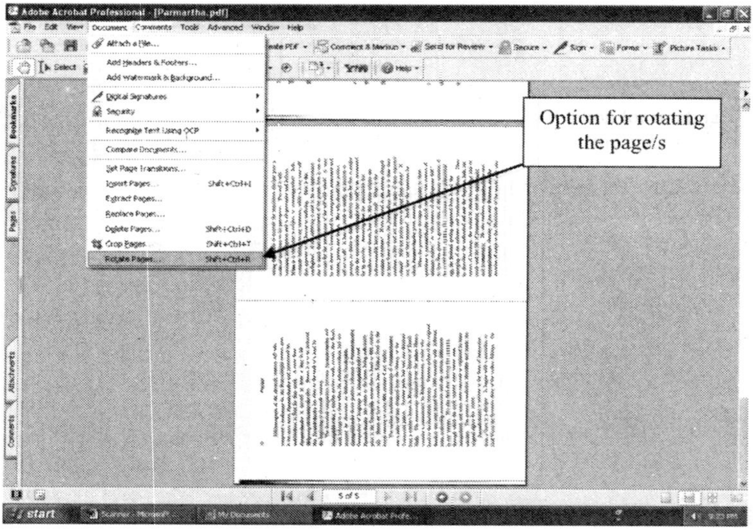


**Figure 4. 17: Rotating the Scanned Pages**

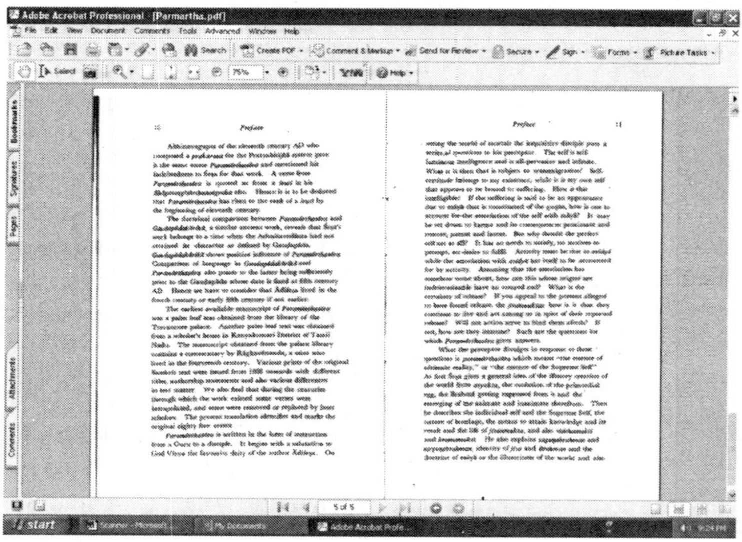

**Figure 4.18: The Pages After Rotating Them**

Then we have to select the option **Rotate Clockwise** or **right 90°**. And the pages will be rotated as in the Figure 4. 18. We can rotate one page or a specified number of the pages in continuity or the pages in the whole document.

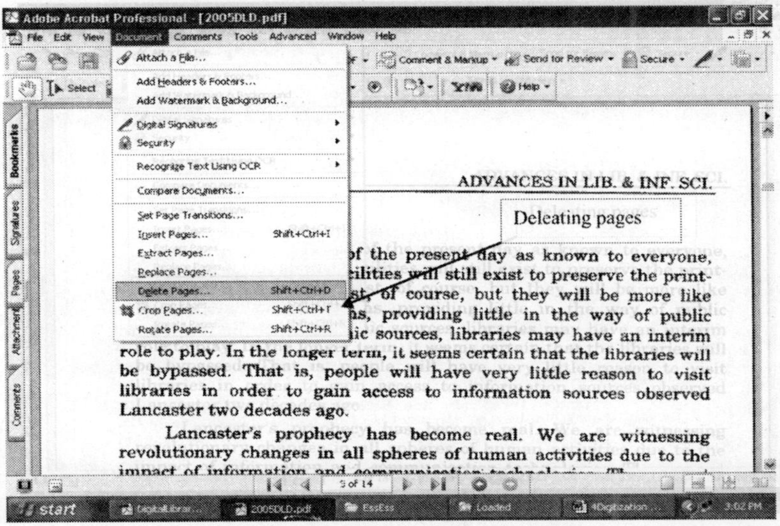


**Figure 4.19: Deleting the Pages**

In the same way like rotating pages Adobe Acrobat has various options for deleting pages, extracting pages, inserting pages etc and can be seen from Figure 4. 19 under the Document menu

Pages also can be inserted later in an electronic book using the option shown in figure 4.20 above. These provisions help to inset missing pages or pages not scanned earlier as remove well as remove duplicate pages incorporated during the book digitization process.

## Optical Character Recognition

We can make text on a scanned image editable. The integrated optical character recognition (OCR) program converts the text to be editable and then places it in a supported word-processing program. Graphics on a scanned image are discarded, or the OCR program might try to convert them and they will appear as random characters.

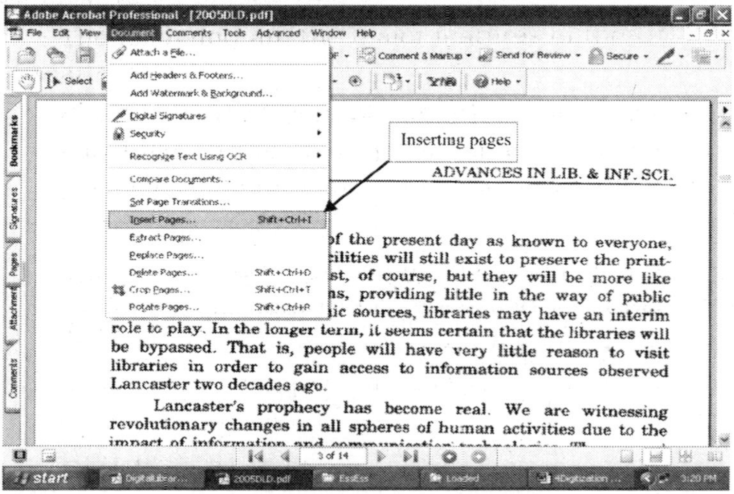


**Figure 4.20: Inserting Pages**

In the Scanner soft ware as per the options seen in Figure 4.5 we can select the output type as Editable Text (OCR) and select the programme to which the scanned item is to be send like MS Word or other world processing software so that the scanned page will come as editable text.

As we have seen in Adobe Acrobat we can also start the Scanner Software from word-processing or image-editing program if the program is compliant with the Scanner Software. Most programs are compliant. We will discuss in detail below about conversion to editable text.

**The Processes for OCR**

The paper documents can be converted into digital images and from that also OCR can be run to generate text.

Optical Character Recognition (OCR) from these images is to be done with an OCR software.

The scanner used for this purpose should be capable of working at a resolution of 300 dpi or above. The scanned page can be initially stored in TIFF or Bitmap format. After scanning and saving as image the document is to be subjected to *OCR process.* The purpose of OCR process is to convert the image and obtain editable word, html or pdf version of the publication. In this process scanning and OCR are completely separate activities Fine Reader is an OCR software with this facility. *Normally most of the scanning software will have one OCR programme like Fine Reader* or *Omni page. They* are the user-friendly OCR programs. *Fine reader* is simple, cheap and flexible software costing reasonably. Instead of scanning as image and then running OCR many Scanning software provide provision for running OCR immediately on the software and then send the document to some word processing software. For this during the scanning after selecting the scanning area as in figure 4.5 we have to select the output type as **Editable Text (OCR).** Then in **Scan to** we have to select MS Word or other word processing software available in the system to which the scanned document is to be send. After saving the file we can edit the file using word processor to which we sent the document.

## Converting a Word document in to a PDF document

*Portable Document Format* (pdf) is the most popular document format for web applications and it would be the most appropriate format for the applications mentioned in this manual. It can provide *bookmarks* that help us to navigate the document pages easily. Once we install *Adobe Acrobat* in our computer and our computer will be ready to convert a word document into Portable Document Format (pdf).

We can use any other *pdf writer* bundled with scanner installation disk, to convert a *word* document into a *pdf* document. Those pdf writers may not be able to create bookmarks in the document. After installing *Adobe Acrobat*, Open *Word, Excel or Power Point* we can open the concerned document and click the **PDF converter** icon in the toolbar to convert the document in to a PDF document.

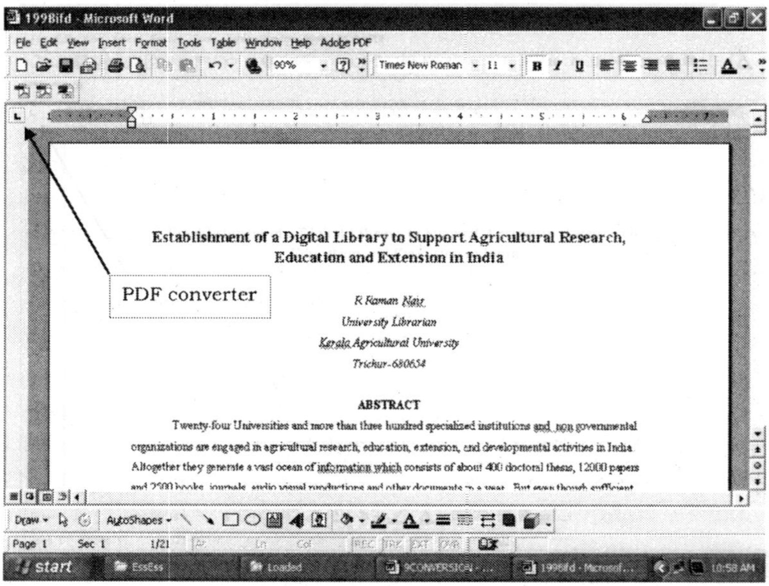


**Figure 4.21: pdf Converter**

Then the following document will it be converted to pdf format and the computer screen will appear as in figure 4.22 to provide file name for pdf version of the document.

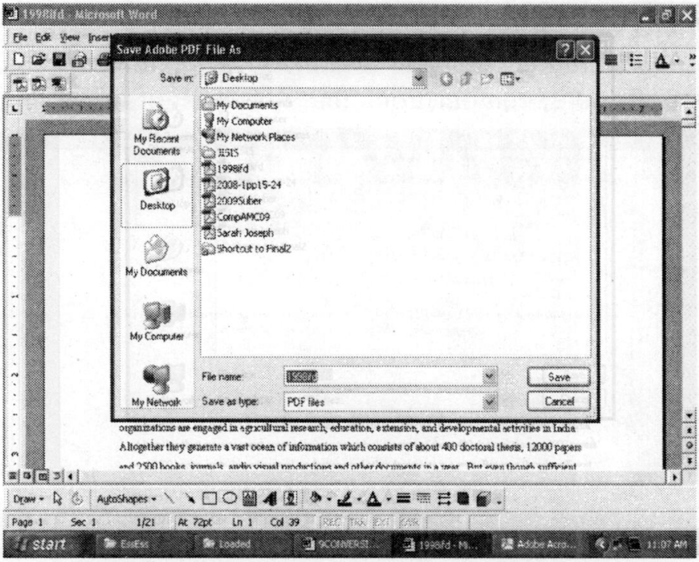


**Figure 4.22: Saving the item as pdf Document**

In the above figure accept the default name or give a new name and click the **Save** button to save the document in the selected folder. Then the program will open the saved file as follows.

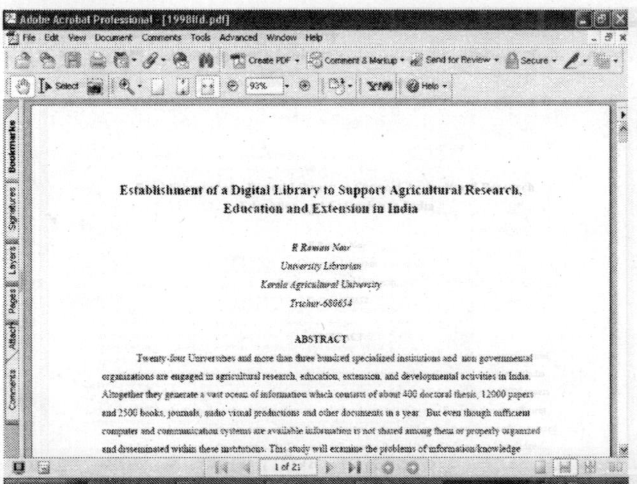


**Figure 4.23: Word File Converted to Pdf**

## How to Put Bookmark to the pdf Document

*Bookmark* in the pdf document helps one to move around in the document from chapter to chapter.

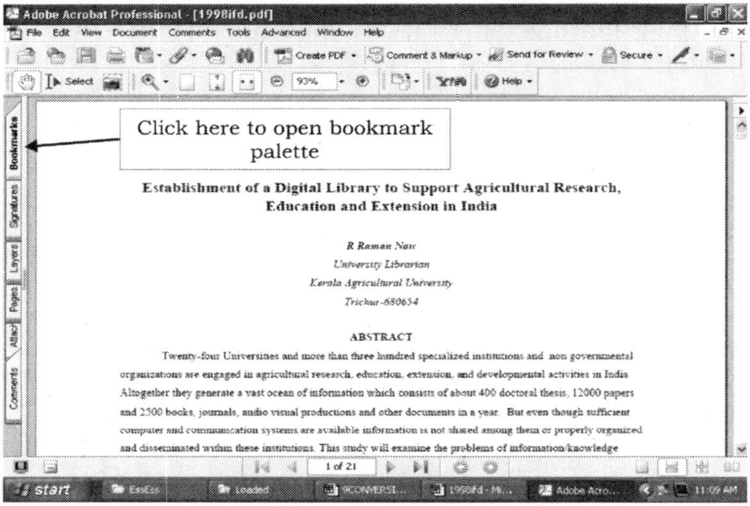


**Figure 4.24: Opening the Bookmark Palette**

In Adobe Acrobat, click the *New Bookmark* menu at the top of the Bookmark palette as shown in Figure 4.24.

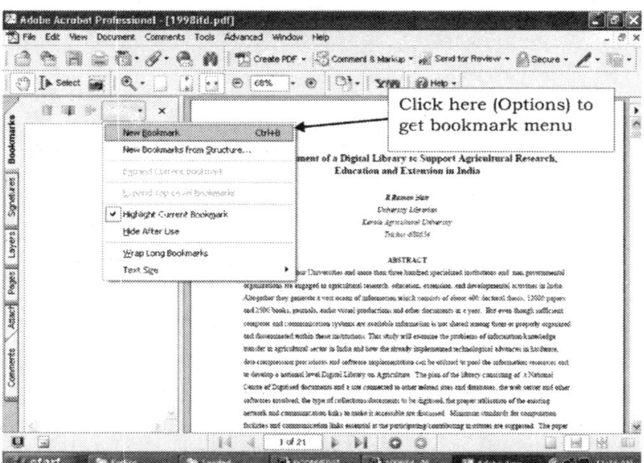


**Figure 4.25: Getting Bookmark Menu**

When we select **New Bookmark** menu, we will get the text entry box for entering the bookmark label as in Figure 4.26.

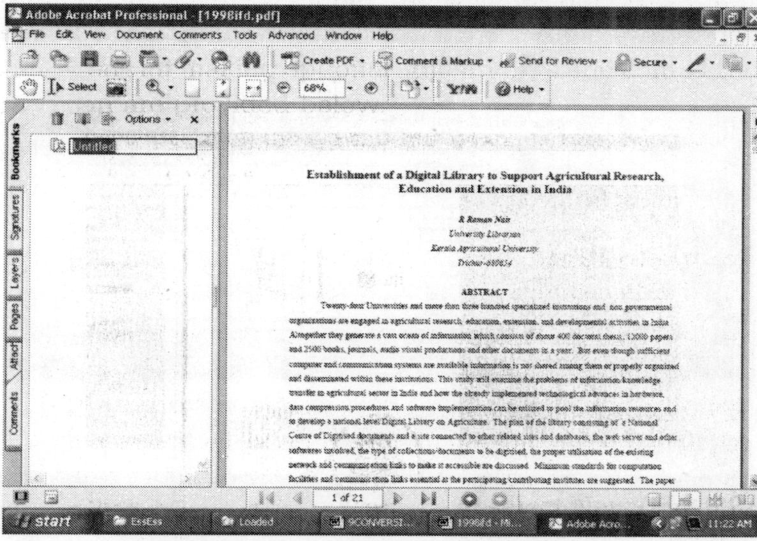


**Figure 4.26: Text Entry Box for Bookmark Label**

To provide a *bookmark* for a page, place the page visible, type the text for the bookmark label in the text entry box, and press **Enter.** To provide the *New bookmark* for another page/ chapter, move the scroll bar on to the selected page /chapter. Keep the page visible, click the *new bookmark* menu at the top of the Bookmark palette. Then type the bookmark label in the text box and press Enter. The bookmark label for the page will appear as in Figure 4.27.

A pdf document with bookmarks provides easy navigation among the pages/chapters.

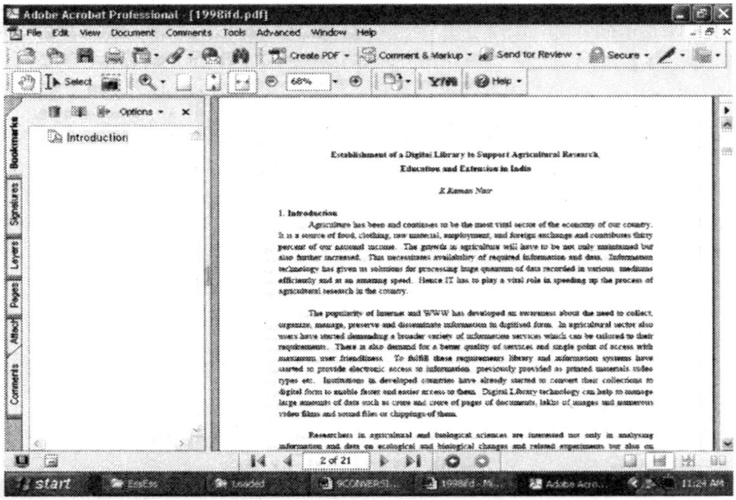


**Figure 4.27: Bookmark Label**

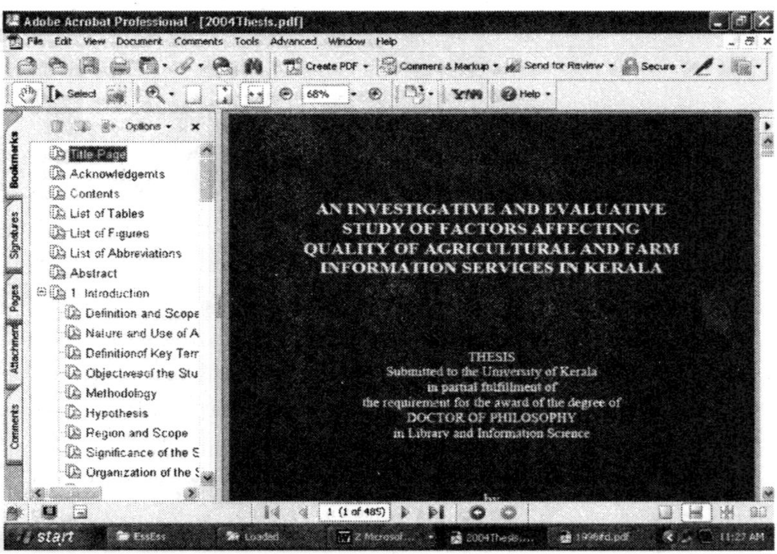


**Figure 4.28: Sample pdf Document with Bookmarks**

When bookmarks are available, by clicking on the concerned Chapter or its sub section in the book mark we can reach the specific portion without turning the pages as in figure 4.29.

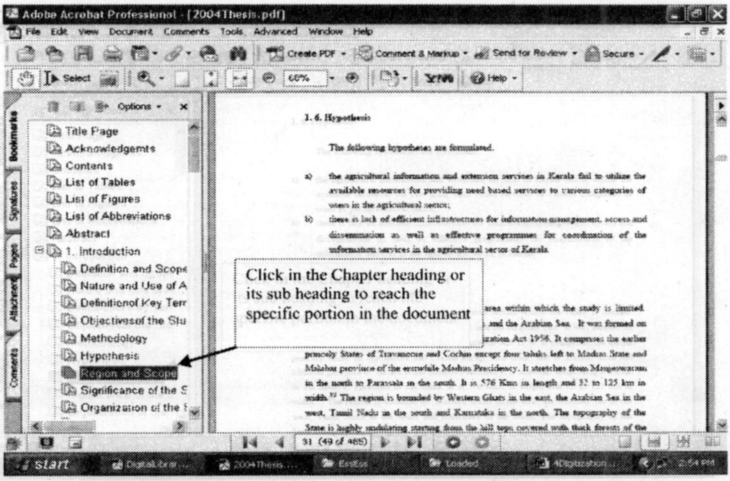


**Figure 4.29: Selecting the Specific Portion in the pdf Document for Access**

A pdf document can be opened with bookmarks by default?

Even if we provide bookmark to a document, it may not show the bookmark automatically when opened, unless we make it as its default property. It is always better to have the document opened with bookmarks.

Click on **File ⇒ Document Properties ⇒ Initial View ⇒ Show Bookmark panel and Page** as in Figure 4.30.

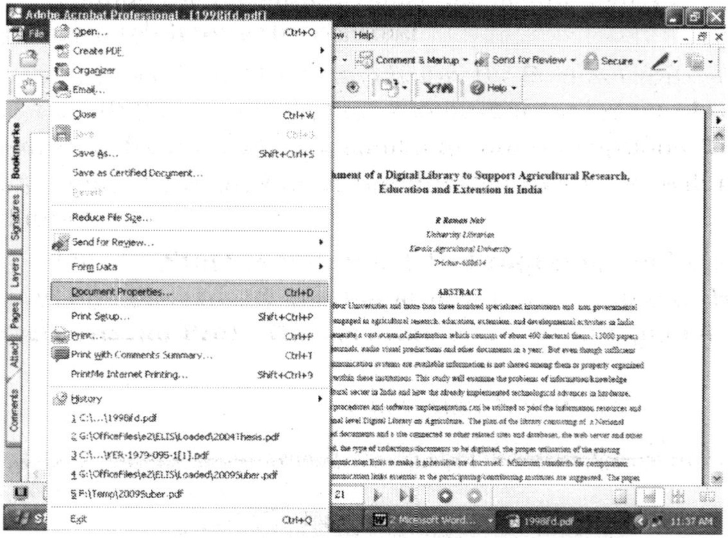

**Figure 4.30: Selecting Document Properties Window**

Then we will get the following screen.

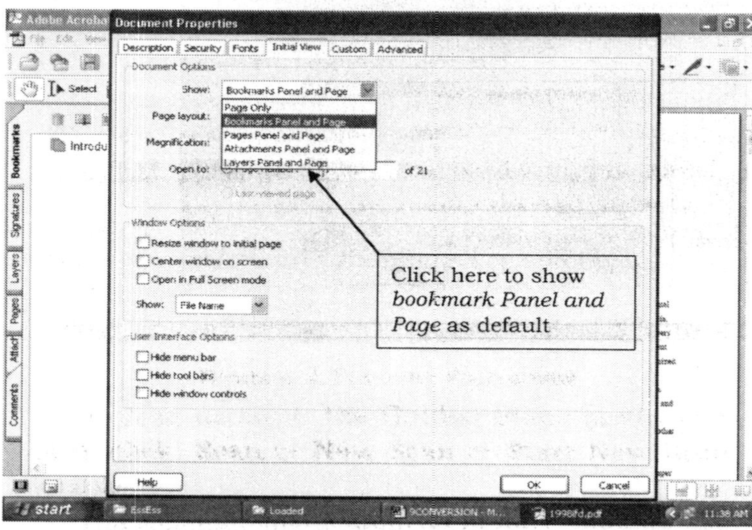


**Figure 4.31: Selecting Bookmark View as Default**

In the above screen, *select* **Bookmarks and Page** and click the **Ok** button to make the pdf document open with bookmark window.

WINISIS the Windows version of CDS/ISIS is a software package for generalized Information Storage and Retrieval systems developed, maintained and distributed by UNESCO. CDS/ISIS is an acronym which stands for Computerized Documentation Service / Integrated Set of Information Systems. Versions have been produced in Arabic, Chinese, English, French, German, Portuguese, Russian and Spanish amongst other languages. UNESCO makes the software available free for non-commercial purposes. This Chapter will cover:

# 5 WINISIS

- Installation
- Field Definition
- Data entry Worksheet
- Print Format
- Field Selection Table
- Data Entry
- Full text Link
- Search Provisions

# WINISIS

## DOCUMENT ARCHIVING WITH WINISIS

CDS/ISIS for Windows (WINISIS) is an application for information management developed by UNESCO. This Chapter will introduce WINISIS, its installation, defining database, and creation of Digital Document Archives with WINISIS

### WINISIS: the Windows Version of CDS/ISIS

CDS/ISIS for Windows (WWINISIS) is a flexible, easy to use and menu-driven generalized information storage and retrieval package. The software is designed specifically for creating and managing textual databases. WINISIS has capability to create any number of databases with different fields for numeous applications. WINISIS application can be used by anyone having a reasonable computer experience.

### WINISIS Database: Key Components

A database is an organized set of records. Each *record* in a database may contain one or more *fields*. A *Field* in a record carries *data element*. In WINISIS, the database will have a *master file* (eg cds.mst) containing all the records in the database. An *inverted file* automatically created during the creation of database will function as an index to the *master file* for speedy retrieval of any record.

In order to create a WINISIS database with any chosen field, you need to define the following components.

**Field Definition Table (FDT) :** The FDT defines the fields such as Title, Author, Publisher, Keywords etc. of the records in the database and their characteristics. FDT determines the nature of data entry worksheet.

**Data Entry Worksheet :** The worksheet is the layout used to create and/or update the records of the database. It is used for data entry.

**Print Format (PFT) :** The PFT is the format for display or printing of records.

**Field Selection Table (FST) :** FST defines the fields that can be searched in the database. The inverted file of terms indexed from the chosen fields, makes the search possible.

**Installation of WINISIS**

WINISIS and associated softwares are obtainable from Unesco website www.unesco.org/isis. You can download WINISIS directly from www.unesco.org/isis/files/WINISIS15_3.exe or www.unesco.org/isis/files/WINISISlicense .html

Double Click on the Wisis15.exe to start its installation and merely follow the default options in the installation wizard by pressing the Enter key all the time.

WINISIS will be installed in the C:\WINISIS folder. *Data* subfolder holds the WINISIS data files. Each WINISIS database consists of around 12 files. Files ending with *.mst, .fdt, .pft* and *.ifp* are important data files. *Syspar.par* is the parameter file that determines many things. Each file in the WINISIS must have a *numeric tag* to identify it. We cannot change the tag number of a field name without resorting to import or export process.

**Creating the Archive**

In order to create an archive of digital documents, we need to collect a few full text documents and place them in a folder in your computer. Create a database of those digital documents using WINISIS. The database can have any number of fields. But our sample database will have the following tags and fields for convenience.

10 Author

20 Title

30 Keywords

40 Fulltext

It is advisable to use an international standard, such as MARC 21 or Common Communication Format for Bibliographical Description (CCF/B) for the purpose

Creation of database using WINISIS is very easy and automatic.

For creation of database, open the WINISIS programme by clicking CDS_ISIS for Windows under Start ⇒ Program. Then we will get the following screen: -

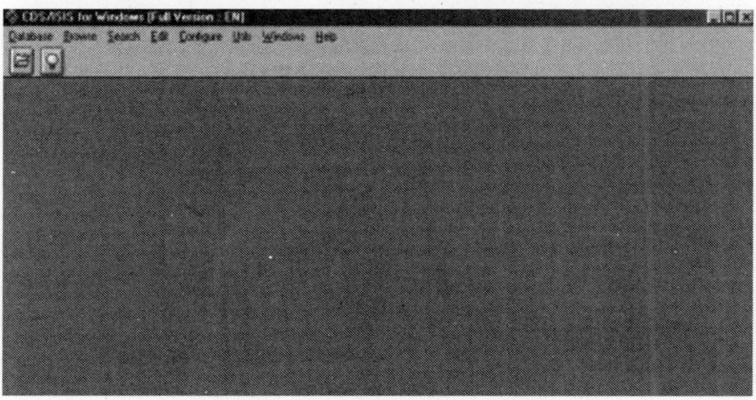

**Figure 5.1**

Click on the Database drop down menu and select New as follows: -

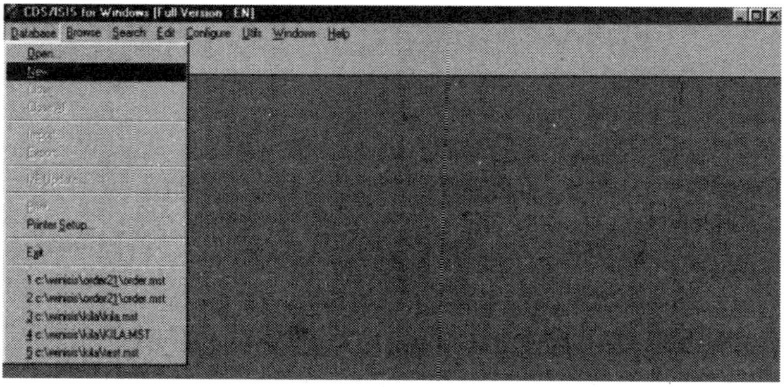


**Figure 5. 2**

Now we will be lead to the following screen: -

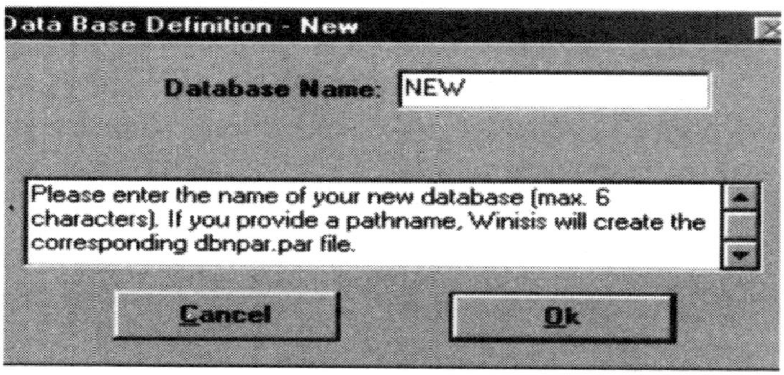


**Figure 5. 3**

We have to give a database name such as NEW and click on the Ok button. Then we will get the following screen: -

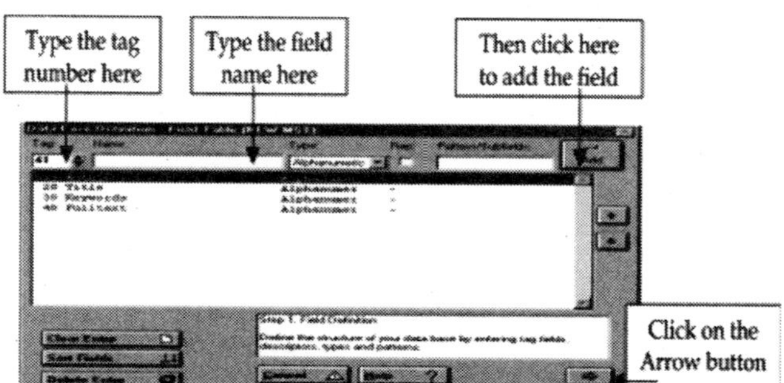


**Figure 5.4: Field Definition Table**

We need to provide the Tag number (10, 20, etc) and Field name (Author, Title etc) of our choice in the appropriate boxes. Beginners may choose *Alphanumeric* under *Type* so as to enable the database to handle the alphabetical and numerical data. We have to click the check box under *Rep* for multiple occurrence of the field, or else leave it as blank. *Pattern/Subfields* can be ignored, if we are not dividing the field into sub fields. Then we have to click the Add button every time on completion of each entry.

On entering the *Tag* numbers and the *Name* of fields, we can click the arrow button at the right bottom corner to move on to Figure 1.5.

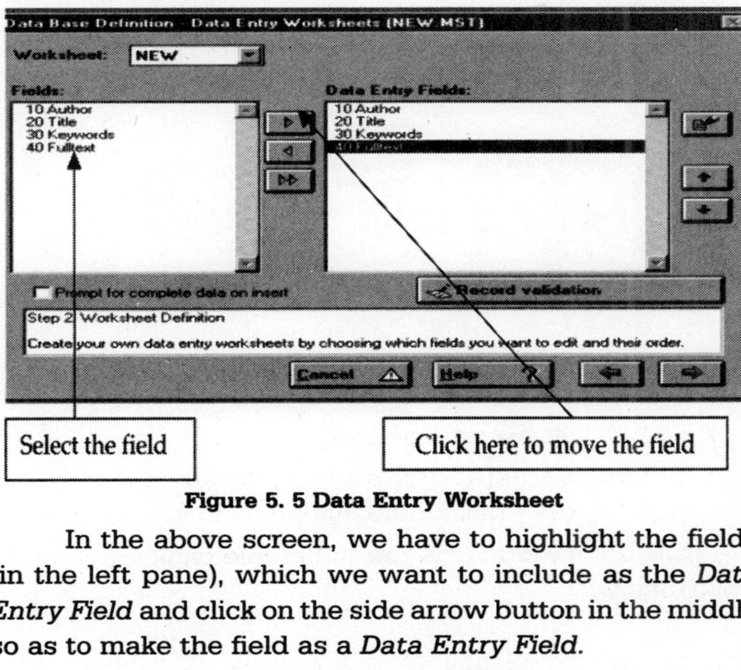


**Figure 5. 5 Data Entry Worksheet**

In the above screen, we have to highlight the fields (in the left pane), which we want to include as the *Data Entry Field* and click on the side arrow button in the middle so as to make the field as a *Data Entry Field.*

If we click on the double arrow button above, all fields will be selected as Data Entry Fields and will appear in the right pane as above. Then we can click on the green arrow button to move on to the next screen.

**Print Format**

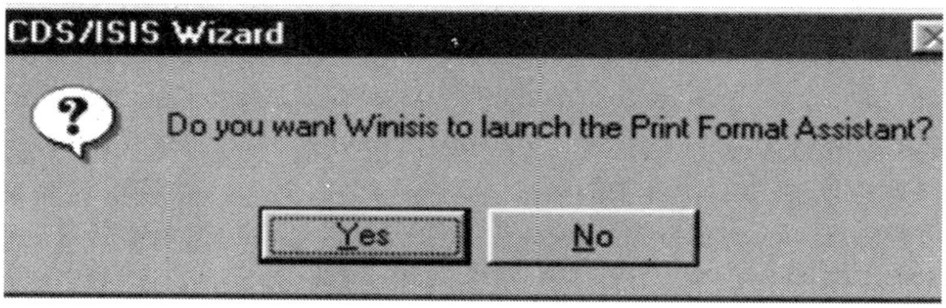


**Figure 5.6**

Click Yes to launch the wizard Print Format Assistant

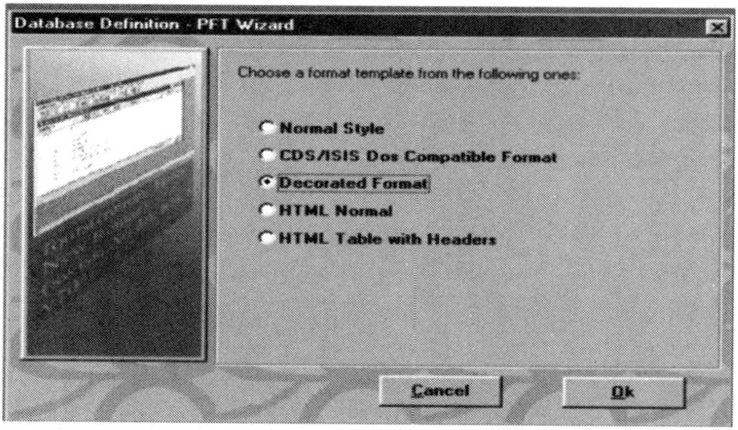


**Figure 5.7 : Choose a Print Format**

Select the appropriate print format and click Ok button to get the print format screen as in Figure 3.7.

*Decorated format* is the preferable choice due to its colorfulness.

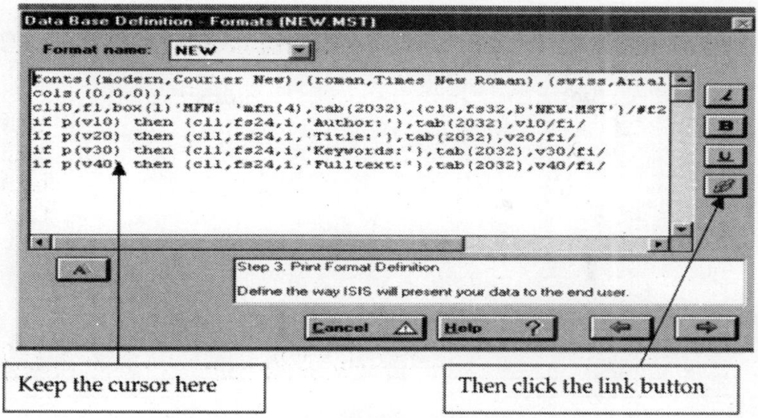


**Figure 5. 8 Print Format**

In the print format shown above, we need to add the following format line in order to appear a hypertext link with the words **Click here**. The hyperlink will be cross-linked to the full text document, if the full path of the document is provided in the Tag **40 Full text**

**link (('Click here'), 'OPENFILE ', v40)**

The basic format for the above line will appear if we move the cursor to the last line and click the **link** button.

Ensure to *provide a space between the OPENFILE command and the single quote*, and the command OPENFILE should be in upper case as shown above.

The meaning of the command is that, when we click on the '**Click here**' link, the click will automatically result in opening the digital document denoted in the field V40, in a new window.

The resultant print format would appear as in Figure 5.9.

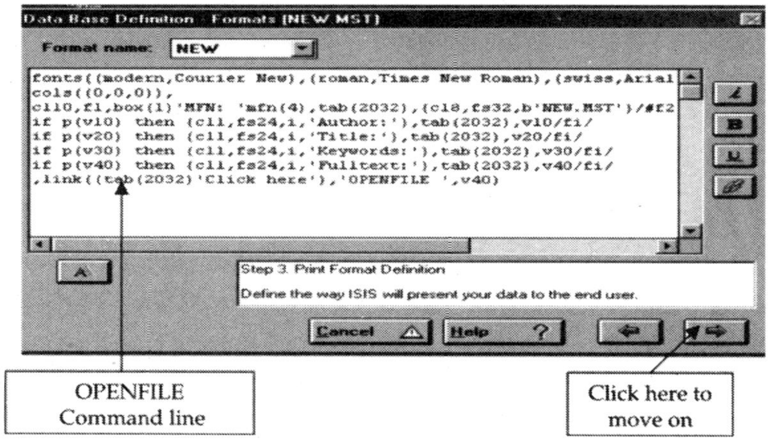


**Figure 5.9**

Click the green **Side arrow** button to move ahead and you will be asked whether to launch the Dictionary Assistant. Dictionary Assistant will help us to select the fields for *indexing* and the *indexing technique* for creation of *Inverted File Index*.

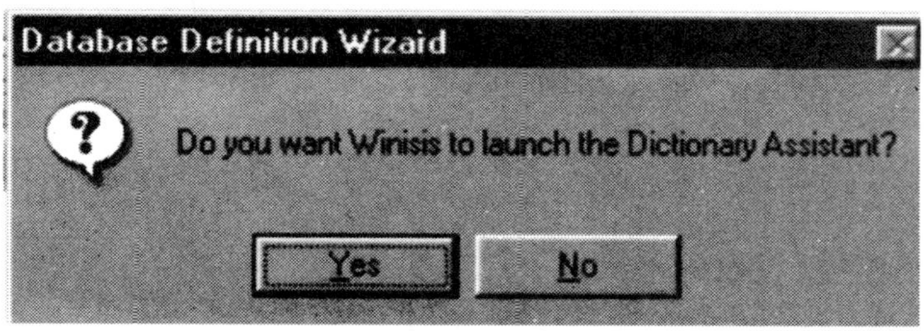


**Figure 5.10**

Click **Yes** to launch the Dictionary Assistant. We will then get the following screen.

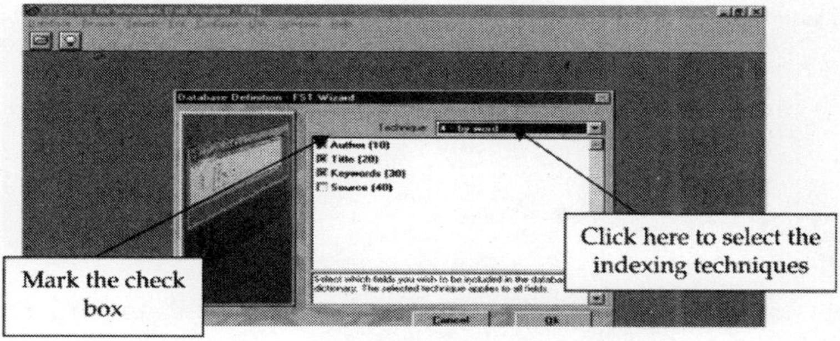


**Figure 5. 11 : Field Selection Table**

Put x mark in the check boxes on the left side of the field names and select the appropriate Technique for indexing from the dropdown menu at the right top. The most commonly used indexing techniques are *0-by line* and *4-by word*. Select 4 by word indexing technique in the drop down menu. Then we have to click Ok to move on to the next screen.

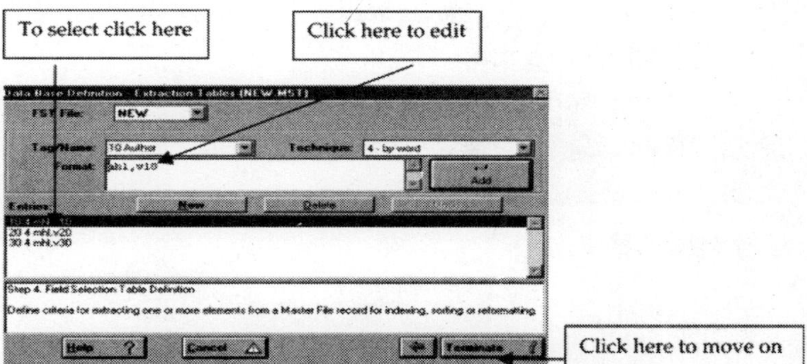


**Figure 5. 12 : Field Selection Table-Definition**

Here we can edit to change the indexing technique. If we need to correct any entry, just click on the entry in the **Entries** box and that will appear in the edit box shown above. We can edit the text, if needed. Then click the **Terminate** button and we will get the following message.

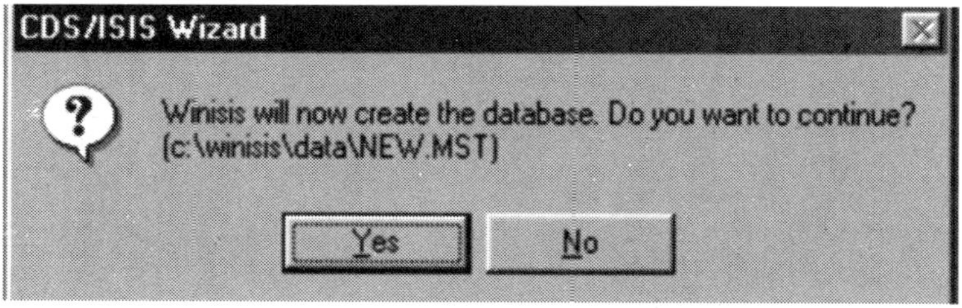


**Figure 5. 13**

Then click the **Yes** button for confirmation and we will be notified that the database has been created.

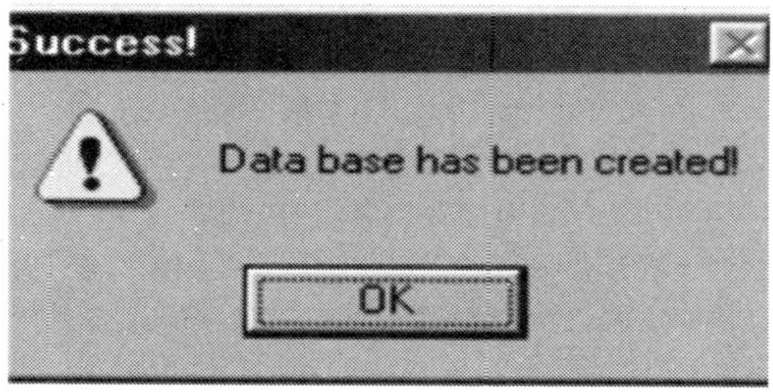


**Figure 5.14**

Click the **OK** button.

Now creation of the database is over.

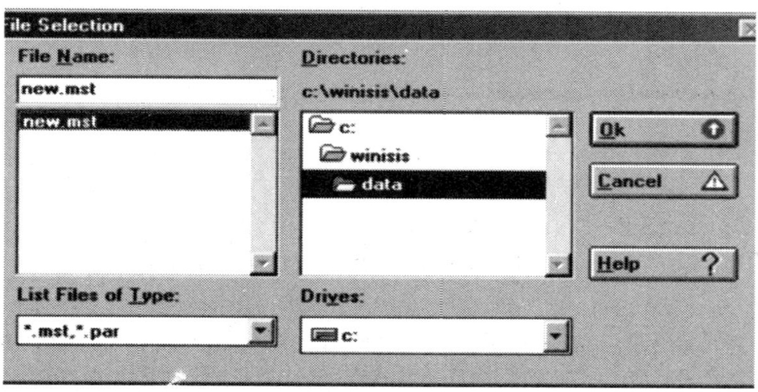


**Figure 5.15**

Then select **.mst** (*new.mst* in this example) file

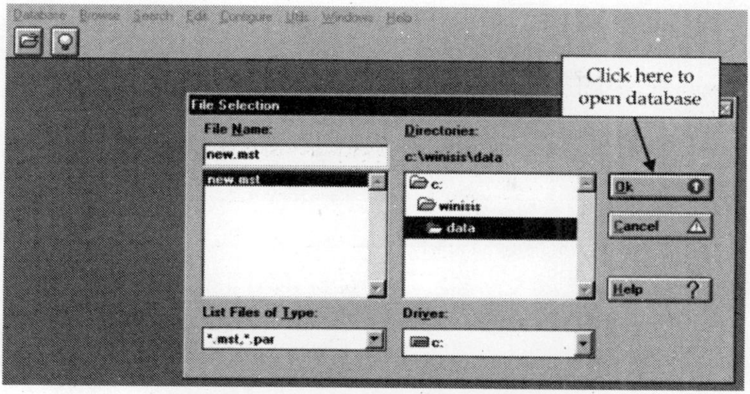


**Figure 5. 16 : Opening the Database**

Click the **Ok** button to get the following screen.

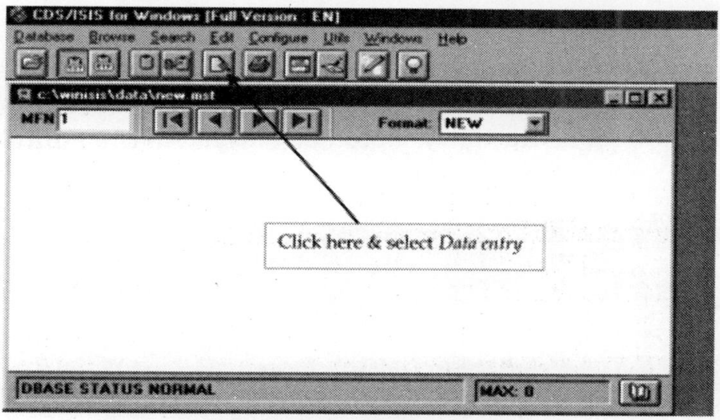


**Figure 5.17 Database Opened**

## Data Entry

Database definition process is over and we need to enter the data by opening the WINISIS as in Figure 5.17 and by clicking the **Data entry** under **Edit** menu. We will then get the following screen in Figure 5. 18.

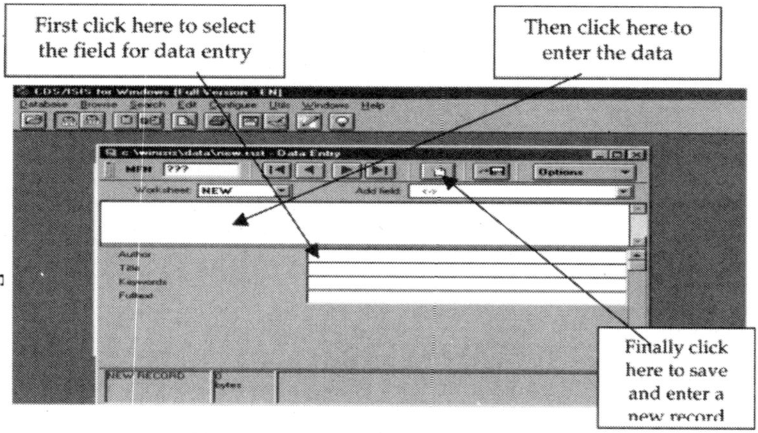


**Figure 5.18: Data Entry Window**

## Entering Data in the Database

Enter the data of all the documents of the digital collection. The full path of the fulltext documents including extension (.pdf, .doc etc.) should be entered in the **Fulltext** field.

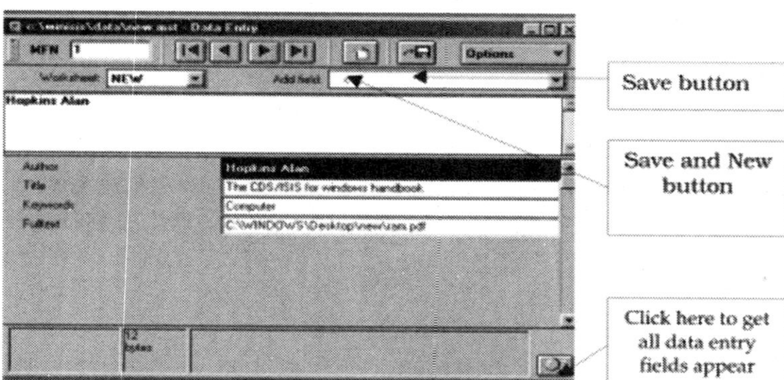


**Figure 5.19: Data Entry Screen**

Enter all the data, save the records and then open the database. The database display will be as follows: -

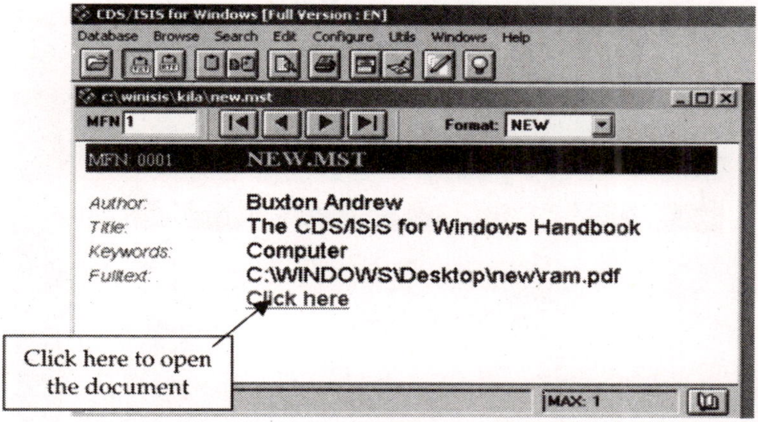


**Figure 5.20: Database Opened**

## Full Text Link

If we had provided full path of the documents in the **Fulltext** field and had placed those documents in the location shown in the field, a click on the link will open the document automatically as follows:-

**Figure 5.21: A Full-text Document in PDF with Bookmarks Opened**

Look at another entry in the archive.

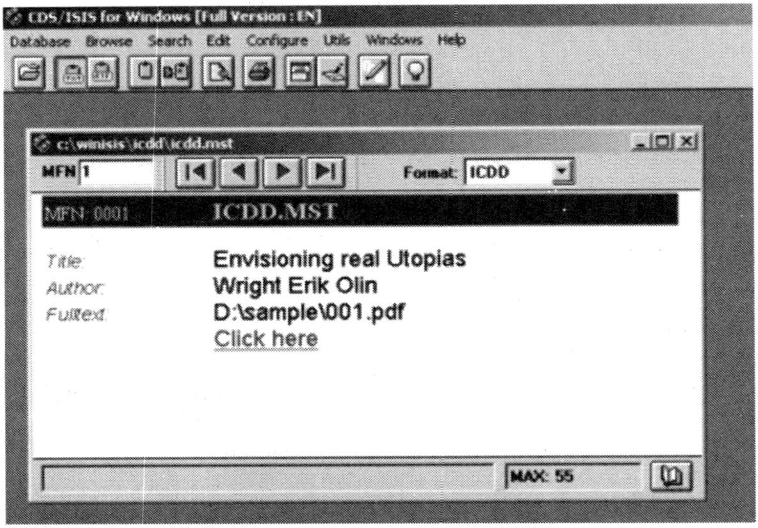


**Figure 5. 22 Another Sample Entry in the Database**

**Figure 5.23**

## Searching the Archive

Open the WINISIS database, click **Expert Search** under **Search menu.**

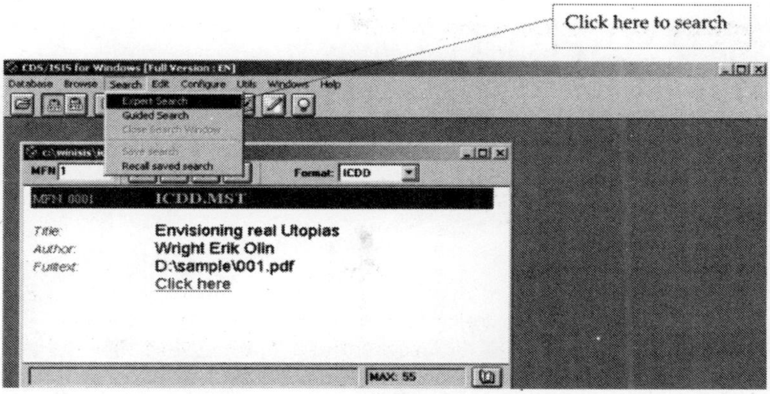


**Figure 5.24 Expert Search**

Then we will get the following search window.

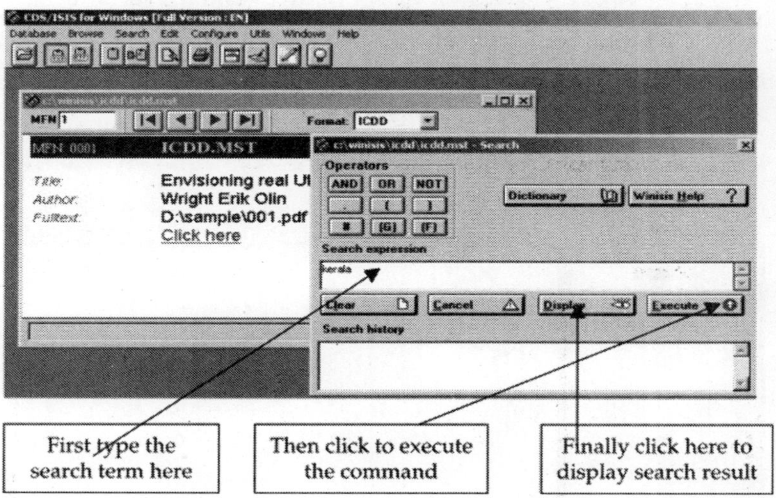


**Figure 5.25 Search Window**

Then we will get the following search result.

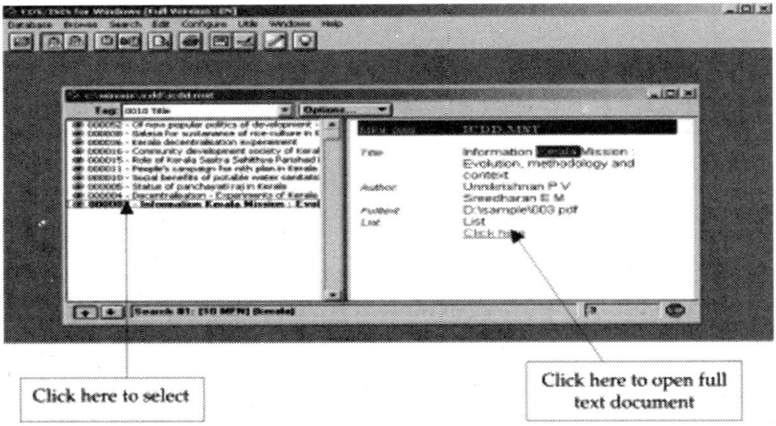


**Figure 5.26 Search Result for the Term Kerala**

Choose the appropriate title from the left pane and click the link on the right pane to open the document. See the opened document in Figure 5.27.

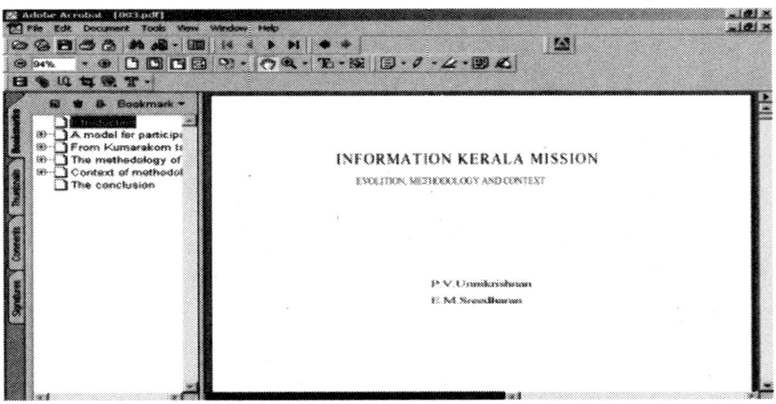


**Figure 5.27**

# 6 GENISISWEB

GENISIS originally developed by the former IBISCUS Association is an authoring software (for Win32) for visually producing web forms to query WINISIS databases. GenisisWeb is the version meant for web publishing of databases. The software is written in Microsoft Visual Basic. Its source code is also freely available. It is Programmed by Pierre Chabert and is available free of charge from UNESCO. This Chapter will cover:

- Apache Web Server Installation
- GenISISWeb Installation
- Designing Query Form
- Display
- Defining Search Page
- Linking Full text
- Testing
- Saving

# GENISISWEB

## GENISISWEB FRONT-END

This chapter explains how to install required software and create a front-end to the WINISIS archives with the GenISISWeb. The actions we will be familiarized with will include the following:

- Install Apache web server
- Install GenisisWeb and convert it in to English version
- Copy the *wwwisis* folder from Genisisweb into *htdocs* folder in Apache, if not automatically copied
- Copy contents (not the folder) of *bireme* in GenisisWeb to *cgi-bin* in Apache, if not copied when installed
- Create the GenisisWeb front end application that can be searched with an *http address*

### Installation of Apache Webserver

Double click on the icon and installation of Apache will start

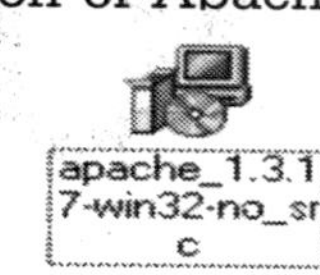

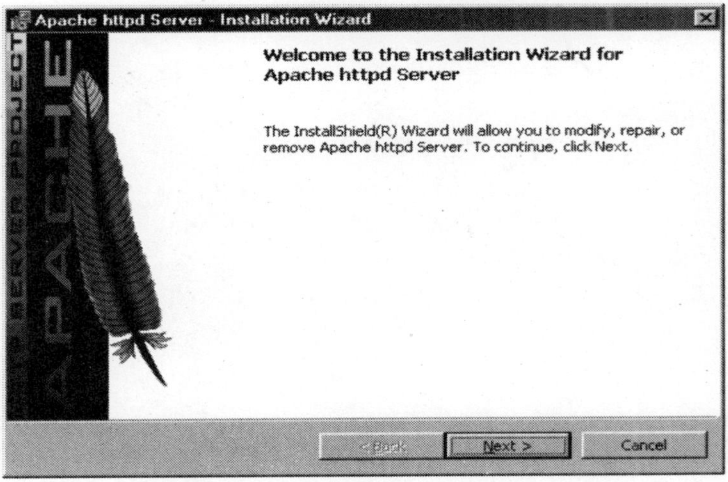


**Figure 6.1**

Click on the **Next** button.

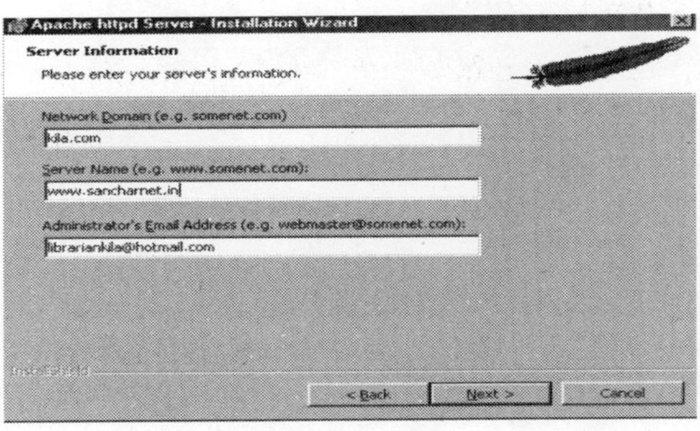


**Figure 6.2**

Here we have to type any domain name, server name and email address. These names need not be real.

Click the **Next** button and the following screen will appear.

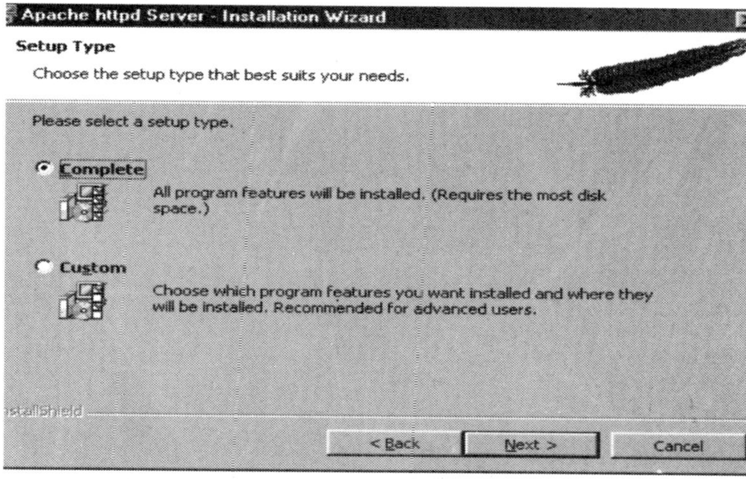


**Figure 6.3**

Select **Complete** (to install all program features) and click the **Next** button.

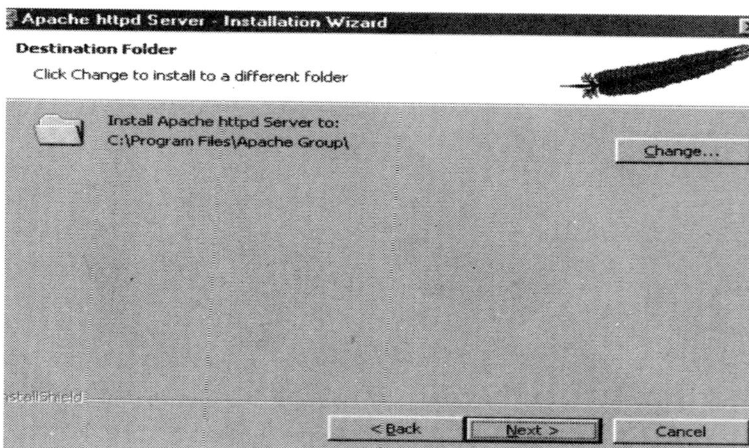


**Figure 6.4**

Click on the **Next** button, ensure to change the path to C:\Program Files\ApacheGroup\Apache as destination folder while installing.

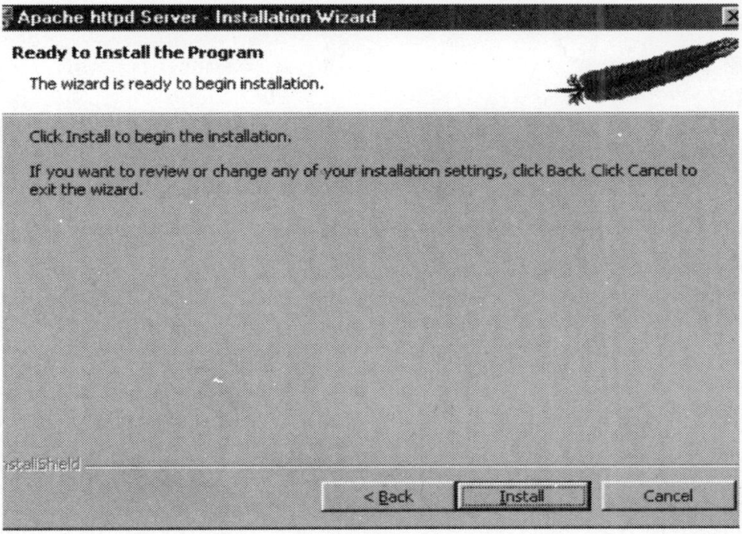


**Figure 6.5**

Click on the **Install** button and we will get the following screen.

**Figure 6.6**

Click the **Finish** button, when the installation process is completed.

Once Apache is installed, we can start installing GenisisWeb.

**Installation of Genisis Web**

Download the GenisisWeb program from www.scribnet.org website or Unesco website and unzip the downloaded file.

**GenisisWeb zip file**

**GenisisWeb Unzipped file**

Double click on the **setup.exe** file in the unzipped items

When we double click *setup.exe*, an installation wizard will appear and we can install the program by opting the default values, by pressing the return key all the time till the installation over.

Then we will get the first screen in the installation process as in Figure 6.7.

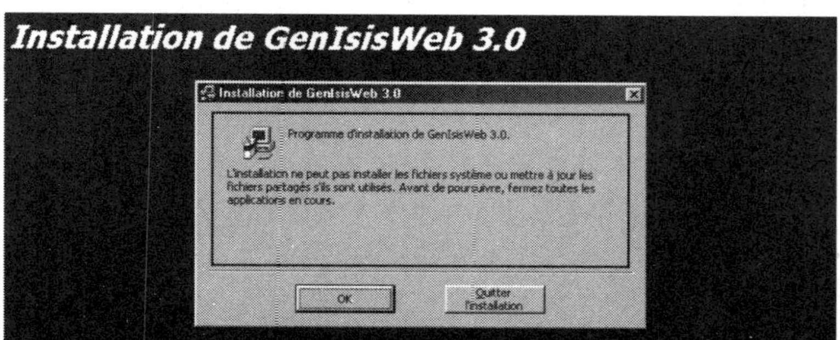


**Figure 6. 7**

Click on the **OK** button to get the following screen

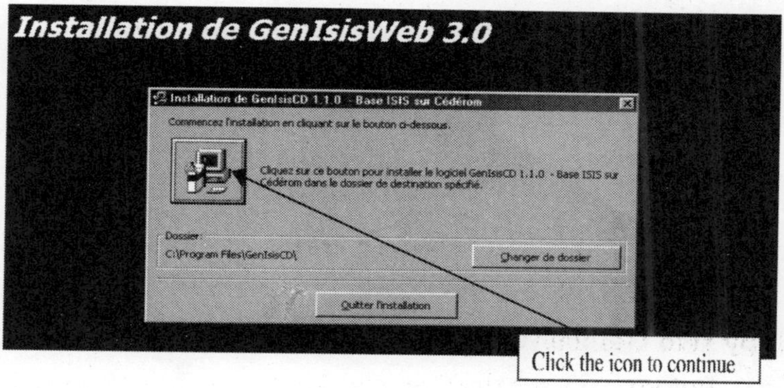


**Figure 6.8**

Click on the **computer icon** on the left side in the screen shown in Figure 6.8.

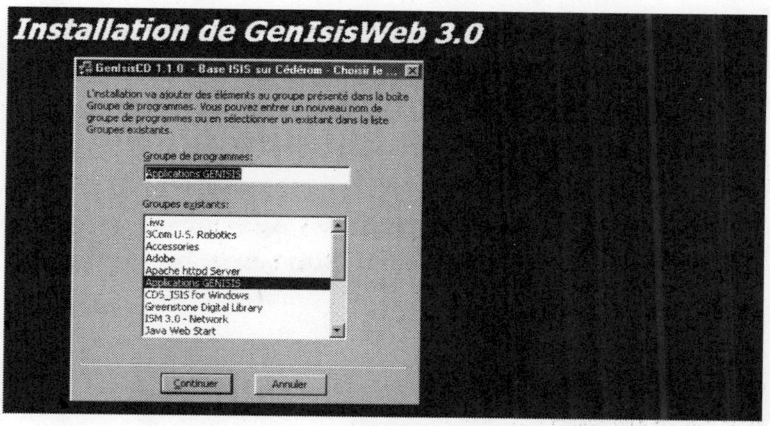


**Figure 6. 9**

Click on the **Continuer** button seen at the lower end in Figure 6.9.

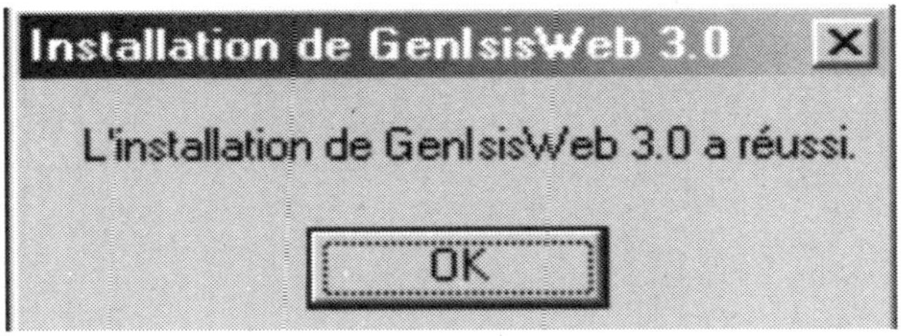


**Figure 6.10**

Then click on the **OK** button to finalize the installation.

### Copy two GenisisWeb files to Apache - A Pre-requisite

Before we start the GenisisWeb for the first time, copy the following files, if they are not copied already.

- Copy the "**wwwisis**" folder in **GenisisWeb** to "**htdocs**" folder in "**Apache**".
- Copy the contents (all files) in the "**bireme**" folder in "**GenisisWeb**" to the "**cgi-bin**" folder in "**Apache**"

### Starting Apache Web Server

Before starting GenisisWeb, we have to run the Apache webserver. To start Apache, follow the steps as follows :

Click on **Start ⇒ Programs ⇒ Apache httpd Server ⇒ Configure Apache Server ⇒ Start Apache in Console**

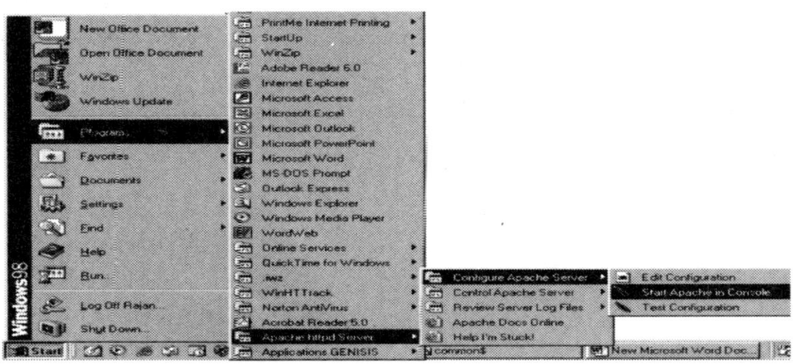


**Figure 6.11**

When Apache starts running, we will get the window as shown in Figure 6.12. Then click on the **Esc** key in the computer or **minimize** button on the screen.

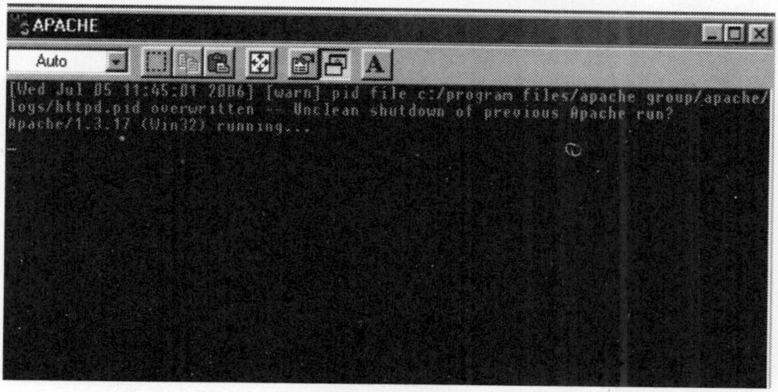


**Figure 6.12**

We can now test to see if Apache is running properly. Open the web browser and type the address "local host" in the address bar and we will get the screen as in Figure 6.13, if Apache is running.

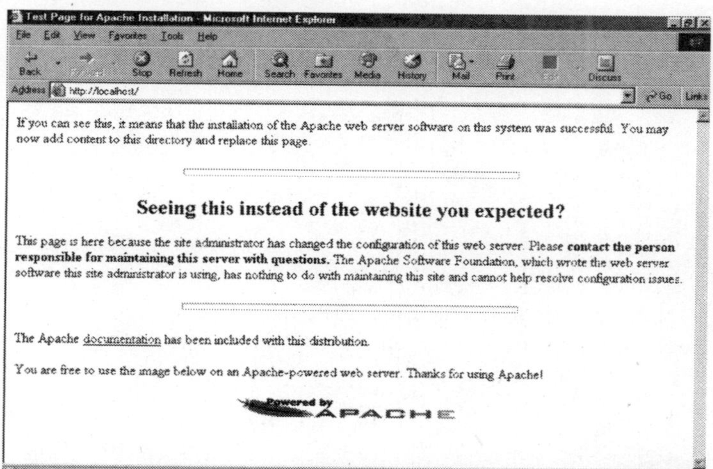


**Figure 6.13**

We can now design your web interface for Winisis with GenisisWeb

## Creating the web front-end with GenisisWeb

### Starting GenisisWeb

Convert the GenisisWeb in to English version, when we run it for the first time, by following the steps shown in Figure 6.14.

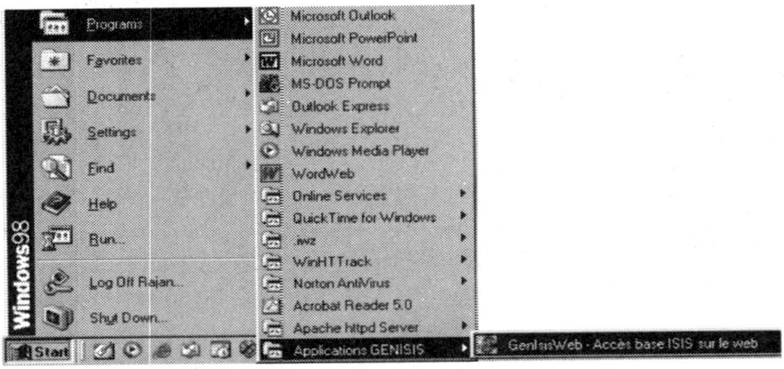


**Figure 6.14**

We will then get the screen as in Figure 6.15.

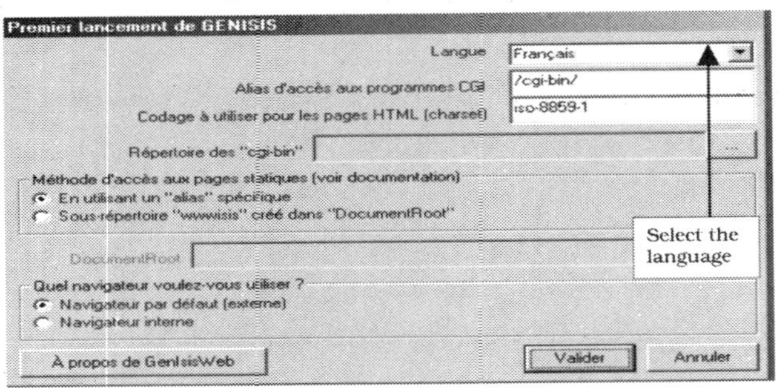


**Figure 6.15**

Select language as **English (Angalis)**

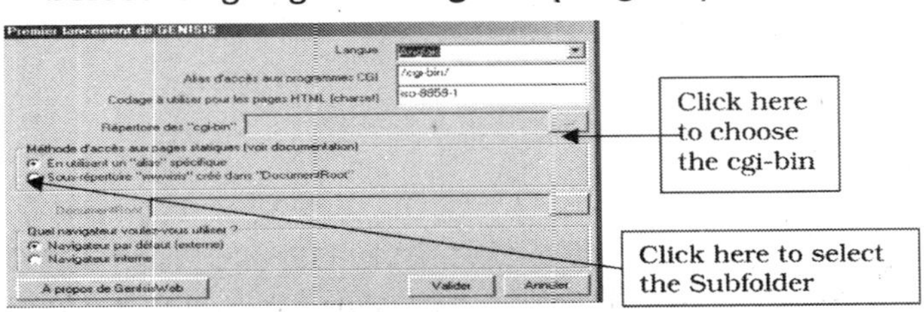


**Figure 6.16**

Select the **Sub-folder "wwwisis" in "Document root"** and click the side button.

Then the screen as in Figure 6.17 with a message in French, asking us whether to use the Apache, will appear.

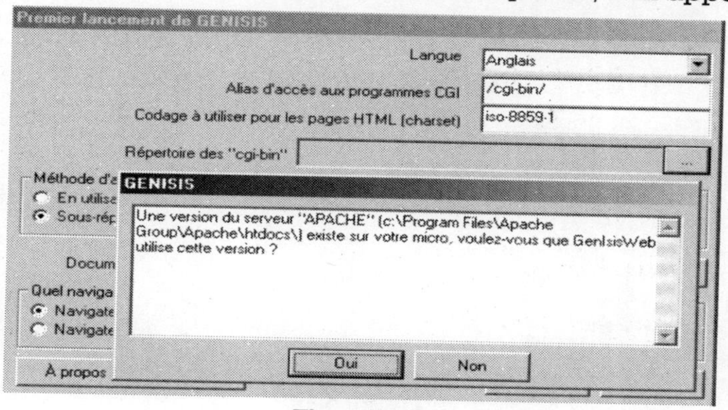


**Figure 6.17**

Click the **Qui** button

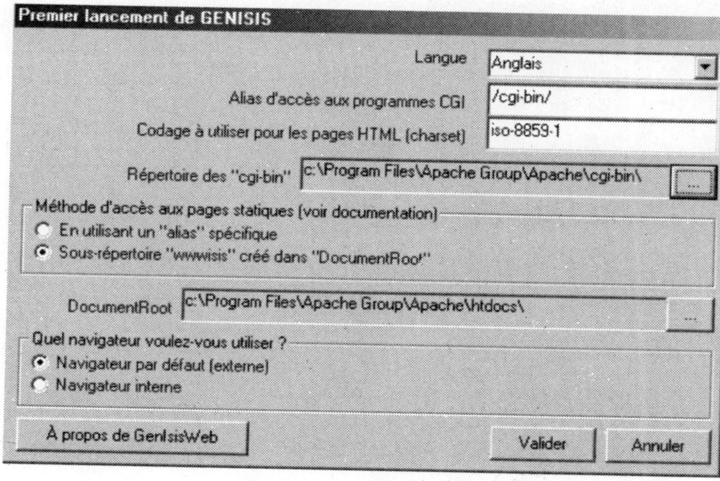


**Figure 6.18**

Click the **Valider** button

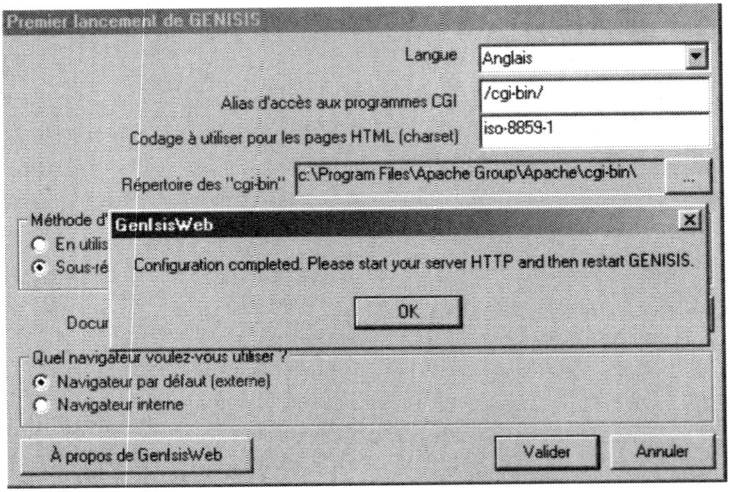


**Figure 6.19**

Click the **Ok** button

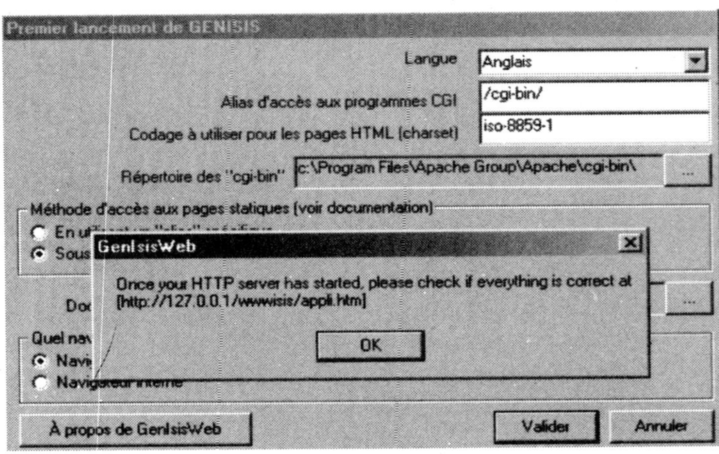


**Figure 6.20**

Click the **Ok** button.

Check whether everything is correct as instructed in the above screen. Now we have to restart GenisisWeb as detailed in the next section.

**Creating GenisisWeb application**

Open GeinsisWeb by clicking on **Start ⇒ Programs ⇒ Application Genisis ⇒ GenisisWeb-Access base ISIS sur le web**. Then we will get the following screen (Figure 6.21)

**Figure 6.21**

**Click on** Application **menu and select** New **(Fig. 6.22)**

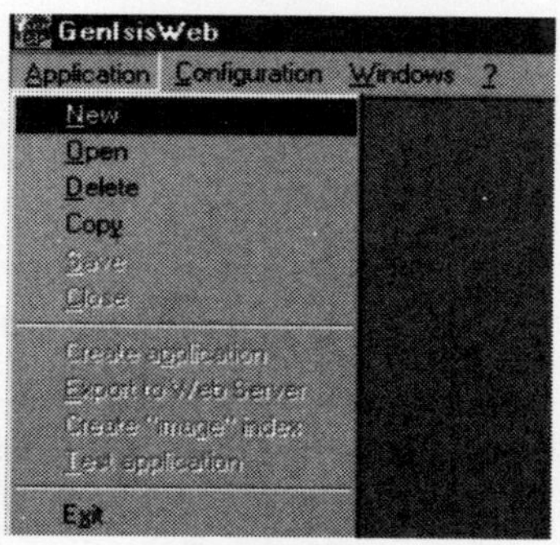


**Figure 6.22**

Then the following screen (Figure 6.23) will appear showing the names of Winisis database available in the computer. If our Winisis data is in any other folder other than in the default folder (C:\Winisis\Data), choose the **.mst** file from that folder.

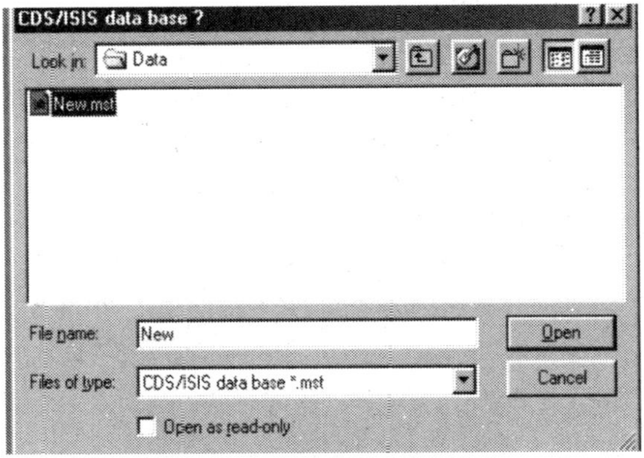


**Figure 6.23**

When we select the database (.mst) and click the **Open** button in the above screen in Figure 6.23 we will get the following screen.

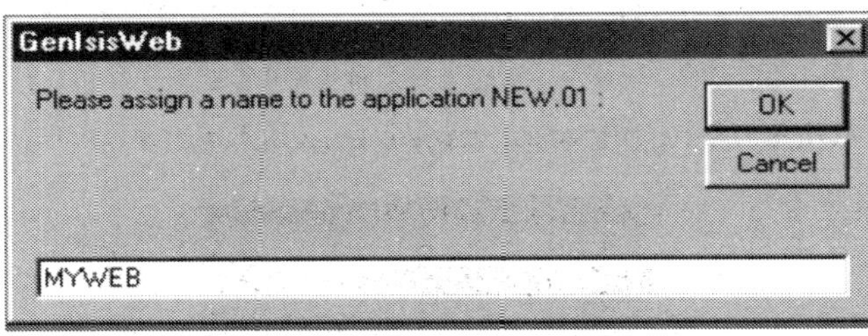


**Figure 6.24**

**Give any name like** MYWEB **for your application and click** OK. We will get three *form design formats* as in Figure 6.25

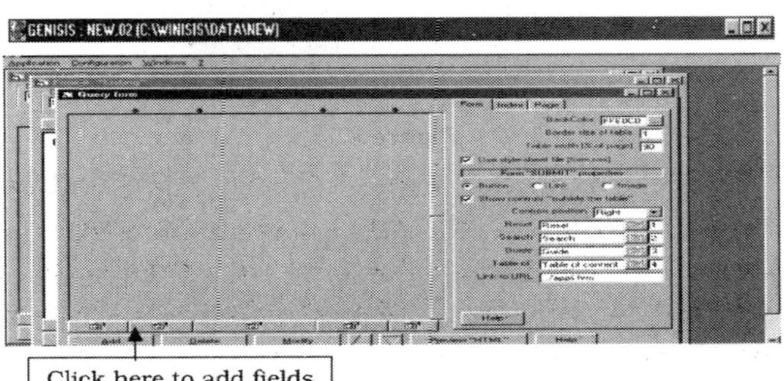


**Figure 6.25 : Form Design Formats**

The form design formats are

- Query form
- Format 'listing'
- Format 'details'

**Query form** : allows us to design the web like *Query Form* - a front-end form for searching the Winisis database.

**Format 'listing'** : allows us to design an *initial display format*.

**Format 'details'** : allows us to design a *detailed display format.* Since detailed display format is not essential for our purpose we have not described the creation of Format 'details'.

We have to create the search page with Query form and the display format with *Format'listing'*.

**Designing the query form**

To design the query form, we have to click the **Add** button in order to add fields. Click the **Add** button at the bottom of the query form and you will get the following screen as shown in Figure 6.26.

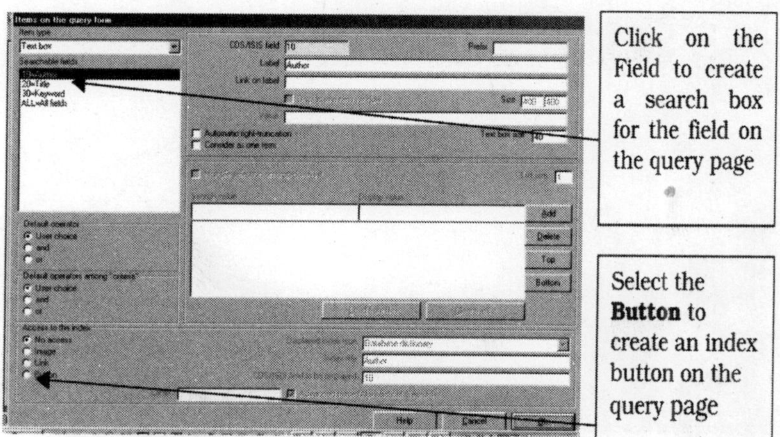


**Figure 6.26**

In the above screen (Figure 6.26), it is preferable to select **All fields** from the left panel (as it allows search by any term in the inverted file index of the database) and then click **Ok**. This will make the query form very simple.

The items appearing on the left panel are the *fields* we had included in your Winisis database. We may select only one field at a time so as to appear that search box in the Query form and click the **Ok** button every time. If we want to select more fields, we have to click on **Add** button and select fields again and again until we put all those fields.

As well, we can select your option with regard to the search operators and the appearance of the *index button* by clicking the check boxes on the left side of the above screen. Index button would help the users to choose the indexed terms.

Now we will get the following window as in Figure 6.27. The screen below shows that **All fields** alone has been chosen.

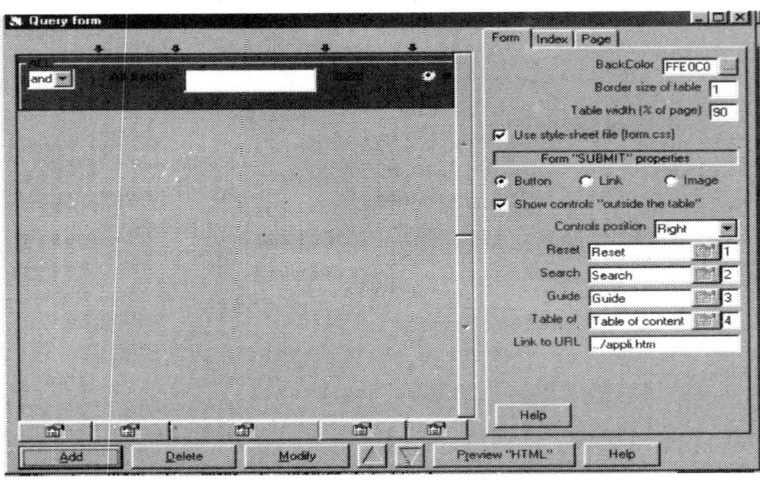


**Figure 6.27**

Select any or all the three tabs **Form**, **Index** and **Page** appearing on the right side of the above screen for appropriately modifying the 'look' of the *Search-box area*, *Index Page* and *Display Area of query form* respectively. We can play with the options in the screen and can choose anything we prefer to have a beautiful look for our web front end. We can change background color and font parameters.

**How to change the page display of the query form**

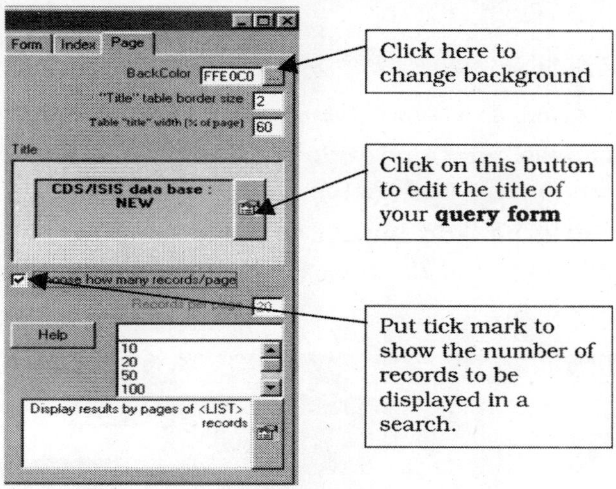


**Figure 6.28**

## Designing format 'listing'

Then click on the 'Format-listing' window and we will get the following screen. It will create a default search-result page, which will display all fields contained in the database, if we do not do anything at all.

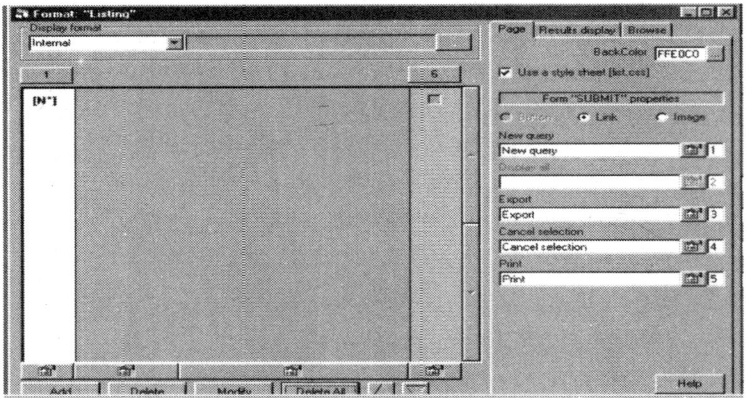

**Figure 6.29 Default Search-Result Page Definition**

Or else, we can design our own customised search-result page with **Add** button, as detailed below: -

Click the **Add** button at the bottom of the screen shown in Figure 6.29 so as to get the following window (Figure 6.30).

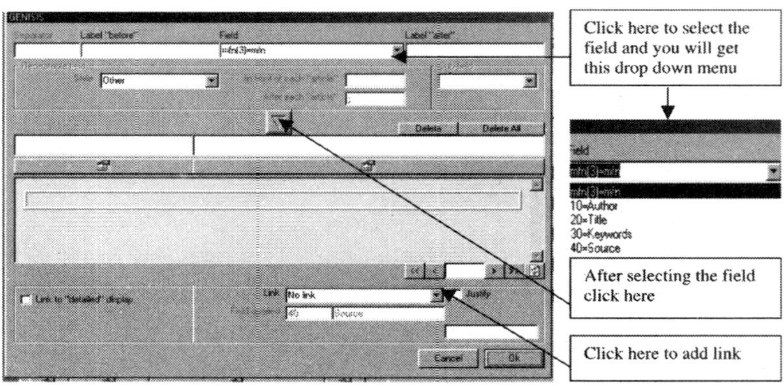


**Figure 6.30: Create Customized Search-Result Page**

In the above screen, select the appropriate **Field** by clicking the drop down menu at the top. Then click the **down arrow** button at the middle and finally click the **Ok** button.

Now select the next *Field* by clicking **Add** button till all **Fields** except **Fulltext** are selected. *Fulltext* field needs to be provided with links, for opening the fulltext document.

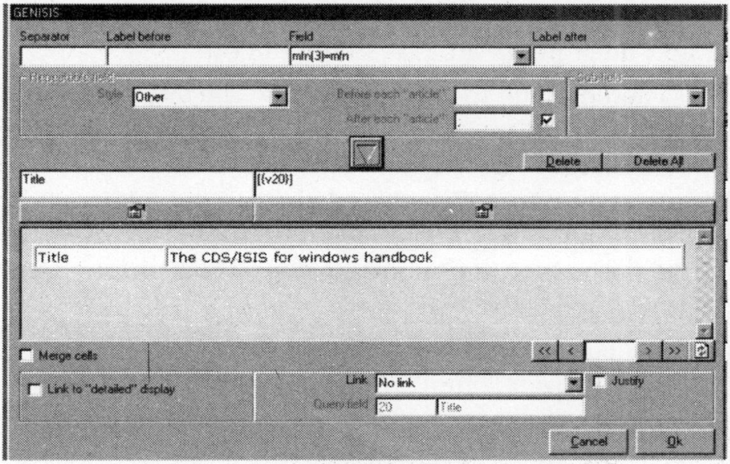


**Figure 6.31**

Now add the **Fulltext** field. The **Fulltext** field needs to have a link to the full text documents.

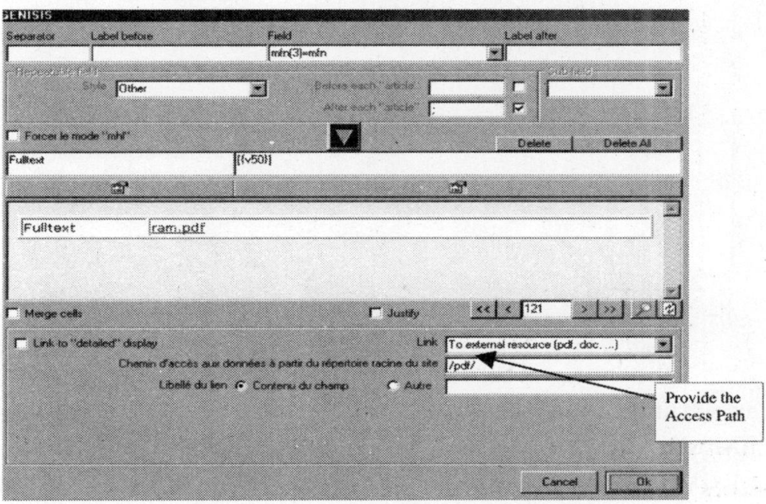


**Figure 6.32: Providing Link to the Fulltext Documents**

Click on the **down arrow** button at the middle as above, so as to display the **Fulltext** file name *ram.pdf.*

Then select the drop down menu appearing against **link** and select **To external resource (pdf, doc...)**, if the full text documents are pdf, doc, html etc.

Then provide the access path to the subfolder where you put the fulltext documents (eg. /pdf/) in *htdocs* ('Document root') as shown in the above figure. Now click **Ok** button to save it. You should create a subfolder (choose any name such as *pdf* for the subfolder) in the folder ...*Apache**htdocs*\\ and copy all the fulltext documents in it.

We can now move on to the next screen in Figure 6.33

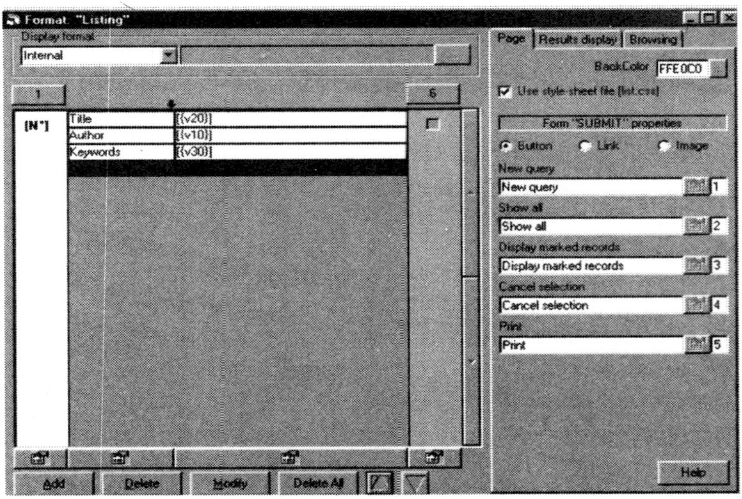


**Figure 6.33**

Designing of two forms (query form & format 'listing') as detailed above are over and we may ignore the **Format 'Details'**.

Create a subfolder (say *pdf)* in **htdocs** and copy all the full-text documents in that folder.

Then click on **Application** drop down menu and select **Create application** as in figure 6.34.

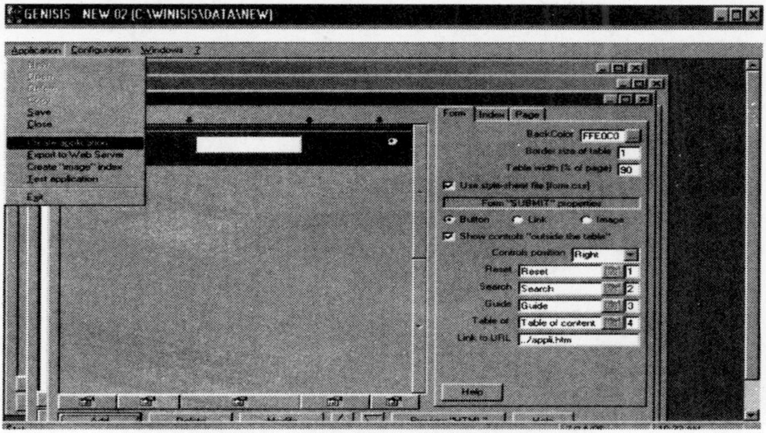


**Figure 6.34 : Create Application**

You will be lead to the following message. (Fig.67)

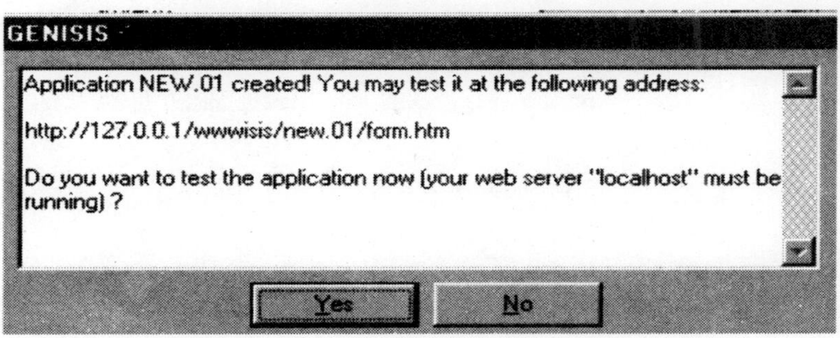


**Figure 6.35: Test the Application**

Click on the **Yes** button and the query form we have created will appear as follows as in Figure 6.36.

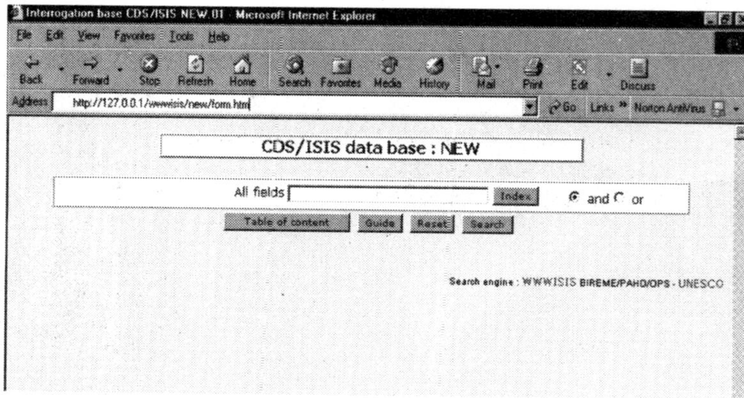


**Figure 6.36 : A Test Window -Query Page**

Type any search term in the **Search box** for all fields to make a search.

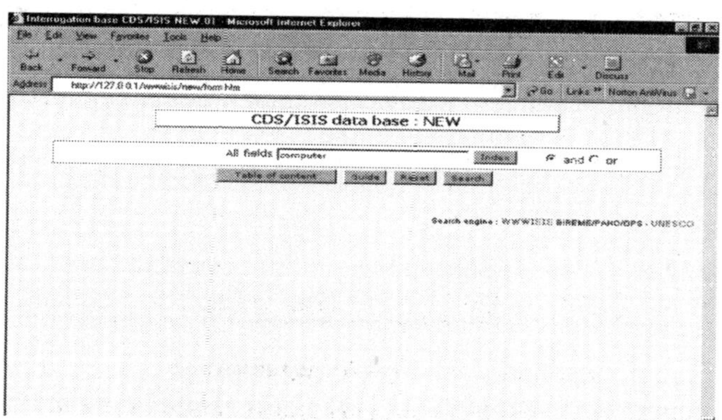


**Figure 6.37: Search Window**

Then click the **Search** button to get the following screen containing the result as in Figure 6.38.

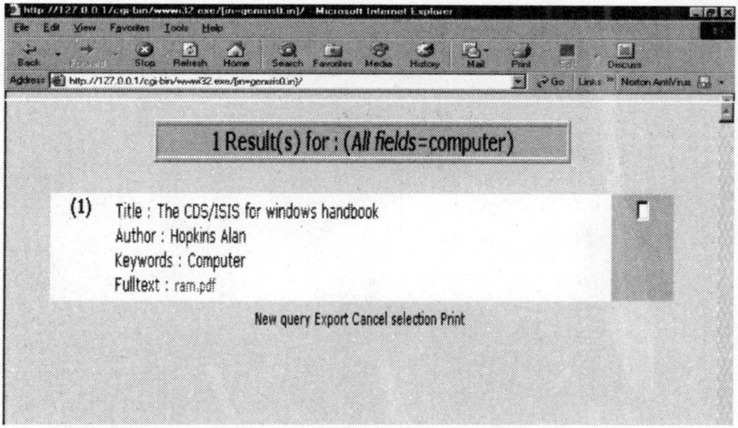


**Figure 6.38: Search Result Page**

If we click on the **link** *(ram.pdf)* against the field **Fulltext** provided above, appropriate document will open, automatically as follows:-

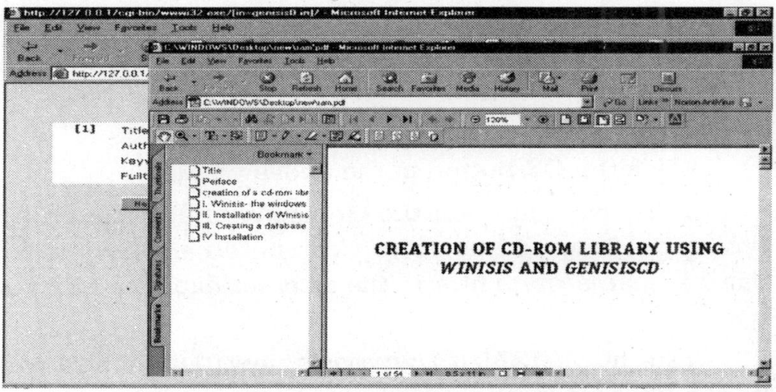


**Figure 6.39: 38 An Opened Full-text Document**

Close the test window and continue as in figure 6.40

**Save the application**

Finally *save the application* by clicking the **Save** under **Application** drop down menu as in figure 6.40.

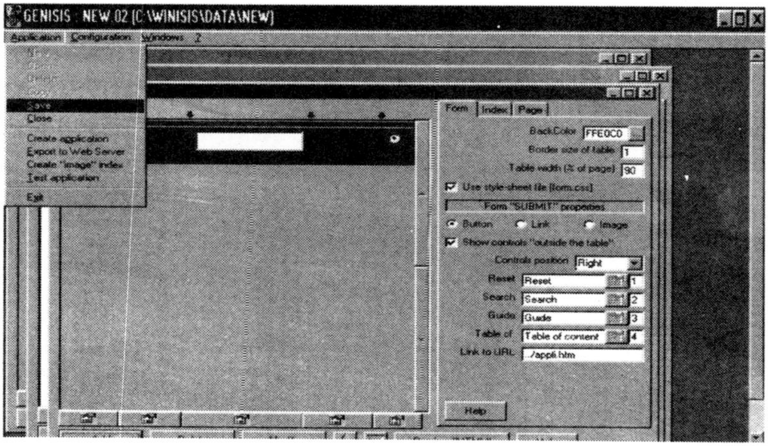

**Figure 6.40: Save the Application**

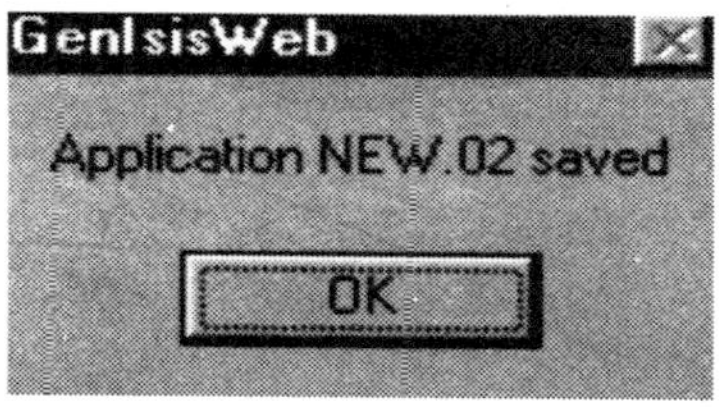


**Figure 6.41**

Click the **OK** button in the above window.

Now, we can open the GenisisWeb application by typing the http address *http://computername/wwwisis/ databasename/ form.htm* in the *internet explorer* address bar.

(Eg. http://127.0.0.1/wwwisis/new.01/form.htm will be the address for the sample application created above. The computer will add .01 to the first databasename and .02 to second databasename and so on).

We can allow others to search the database with the above http address.

# 7

# WEB PUBLISHING

GenisisWeb, is the version meant for web publishing of databases. This chapter shows how the database developed in WINISIS along with the full text archives can be published in Web. the following aspects are covered here.

Exporting to Web server
Choosing OS
Creating folders in Server
Exporting Data
Testing Query Form

# WEB PUBLISHING

## PUBLISHING IN THE WEB

We can publish the Winisis database application in a website by export function of the GenisisWeb software. This chapter shows how our database can be published in a Website.

### Exporting the application to the web-server

Open the GenisisWeb application created in the last session.

Click on **Export to web server** under the **Application** drop down menu as in figure 7.1

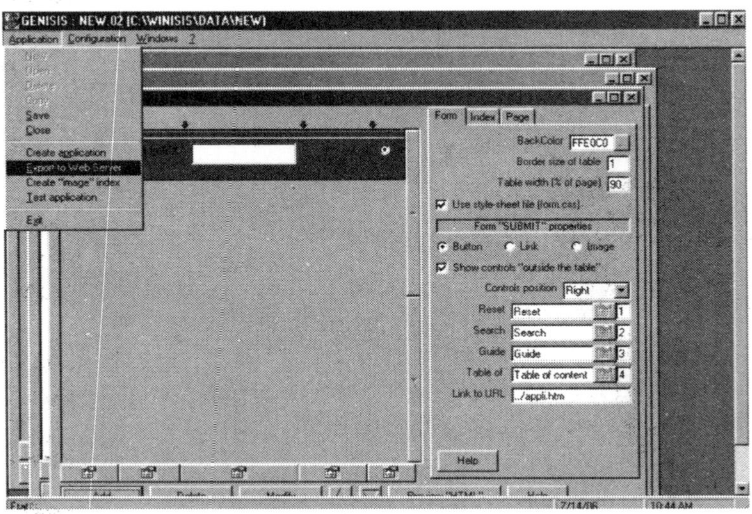


**Figure 7.1: Exporting to Web-server**

Then we will get a dialogue box in Figure 7.2

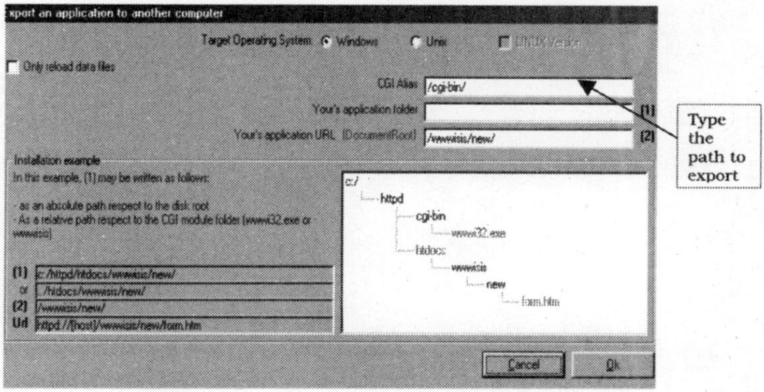


**Figure 7.2**

In the above screen we can choose the operating system **Windows** or **Unix**. Then type a path to export (as shown on left bottom of the screen eg. *.../htdocs/wwwisis/new/)* on the box for **Your application folder** as in Figure 7.3.

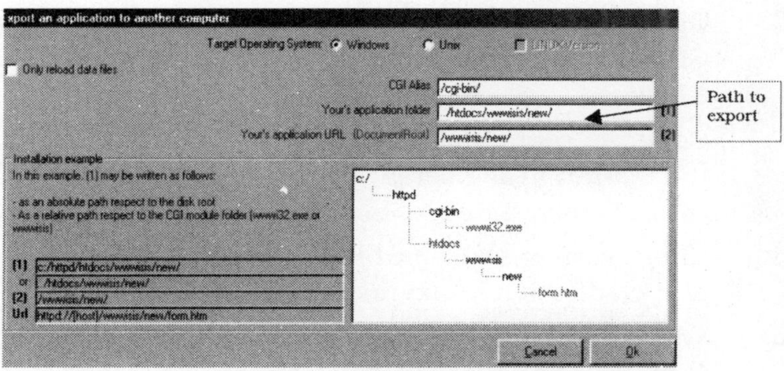


**Figure 7.3**

Then click the **Ok** button to start the export process.

On completion of export process, we will get a message. The message will give us instructions on what to do.

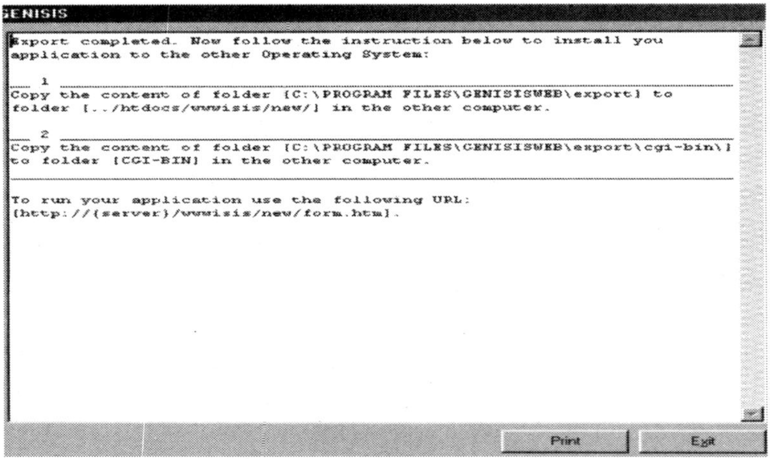


**Figure 7.4 : Instructions**

Then we have to follow these steps: -

1. Create a new folder **wwwisis** in the **htdocs** and then create another subfolder namely **new** in **wwwisis** folder of the server computer (..htdocs/wwwisis/new)
2. Copy the contents of the folder **export** (under GenisisWeb) from the first computer to the **new** folder (..htdocs/wwwisis) in the server computer
3. Copy the contents of the **cgi-bin** (of GenisisWeb) to the **cgi-bin** in the server computer (The contents of the *cgi-bin* will be identical files for any database)
4. Create a new folder **pdf** in the **htdocs** of the server and place the full-text documents in that folder
5. When you type **http:/servername/wwwisis/new/ form.htm**, the query form will appear. The query form allows us to search the document collection.

In *Unix,* the instructions will be slightly different and follow the instructions. When we choose Unix, linux will become active and we can choose it, if our server is linux.

# 8 GENISIS CD

GENISIS CD is a version of GENISIS for developing CDROM interfaces for WINISIS databases. It is now available free of charge from UNESCO FTP site. The software is written in Microsoft Visual Basic. This Chapter will cover:

- Installation
- Language Conversion
- Archiving in CDROM
- Designing Query form
- Designing Form for Listing
- Essential File Modifications
- Finalizing CD
- Testing

# GENISIS CD

## ARCHIVING WITH GENISISCD

This chapter will deal with the Creation of CD-ROM Library with GenISISCD. First we have to create a WINISIS database with *Author*, *Title*, *Keywords* and *Fulltext* fields

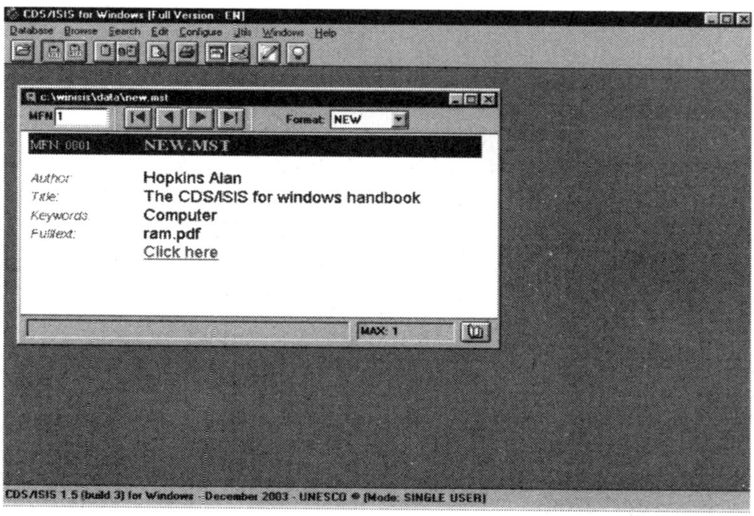


**Figure 8.1**

In **Fulltext** field, provide only file name of the fulltext document.

When the database creation is over we can pass on to the next Chapter for creation of web front end.

### Installation of the GenISISCD

Download the GenISISCD program from *www.scribnet.org* website or Unesco website. Unzip the downloaded zipped file and we will get the following three files as shown in Figure 8.2.

**Figure 8.2**

Double click the **setup.exe** file shown above

Then we will get the first screen in the installation process as in Figure 8.3.

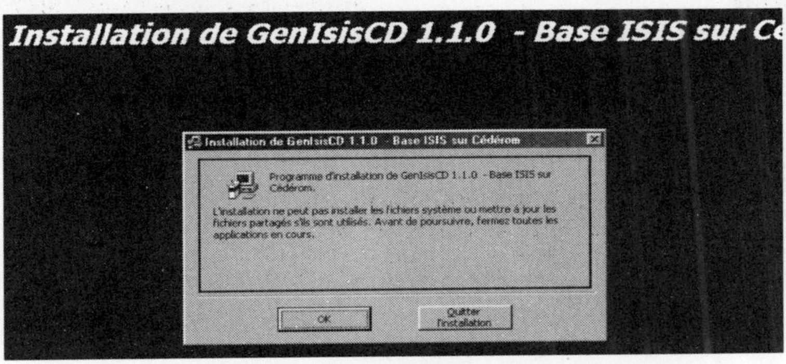


**Figure 8.3**

Click on the **OK** button and we will be lead to a screen as in Figure 8.4.

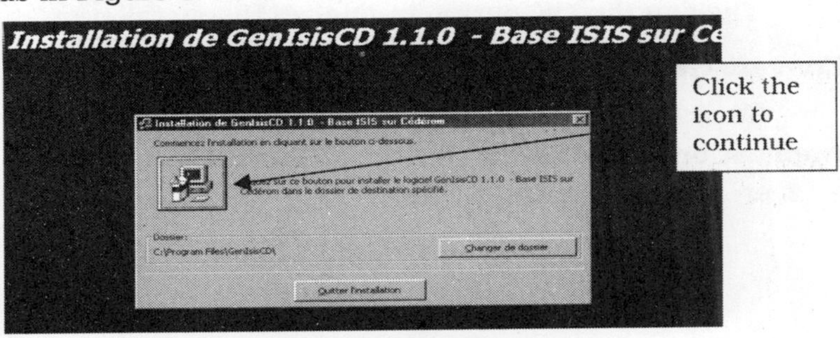


**Figure 8.4**

Click on the **computer icon** on the left side shown in Figure 8.4 and we will get the following screen in Figure 8.5.

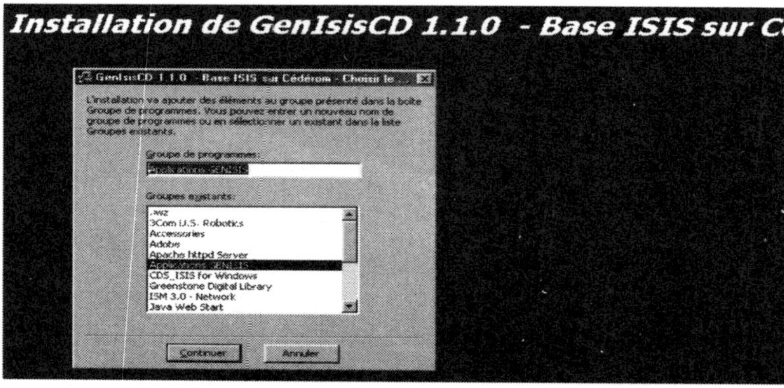


**Figure 8.5**

Click on the **Continuer** button and we will be notified the successful installation of the program.

**Figure 8.6**

Click on the **OK** button to finalize the installation.

**Convert GenISISCD into English**

To start GenISISCD program, go to **Start\Programs\ Applications GenISIS** and select **\ GenISISCD -BaseISIS** as seen in the following figure:

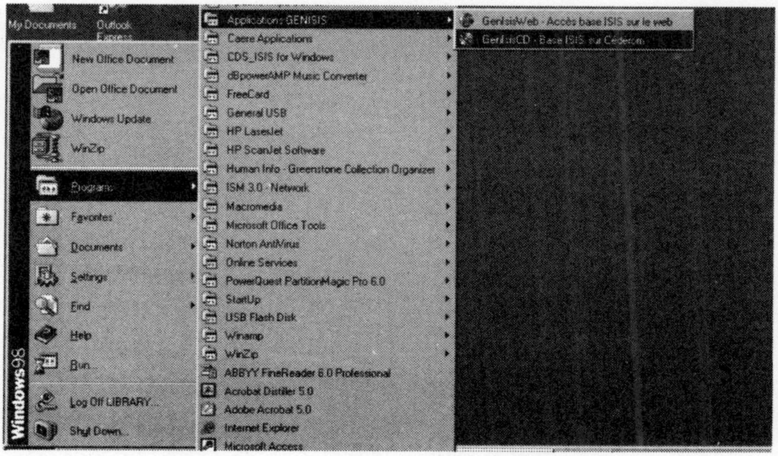


**Figure 8.7**

Then we will get the following screen in Figure 8.8

**Figure 8.8**

Click **Configuration** menu and select **Options** to get the screen shown in Figure 8.9.

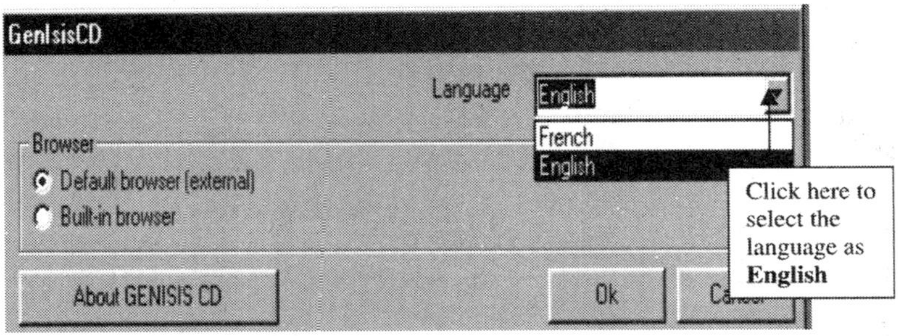


**Figure 8.9**

In the above screen click on the language drop down arrow key and select the language **English** and click **Ok** button.

If our installation doesn't show English language, we have to create a notepad file with the following contents.

**[OPTIONS]**

**LANG=en**

We have to save it with the name **GenISISCD** and put it in our folder C:\Program Files\GenISISCD

The application will be converted to English when we refresh it.

When we reopen the program it will appear in English as in figure 8.10..

### Creating CD-ROM Library

Click on **Application** menu and select **new** as follows.

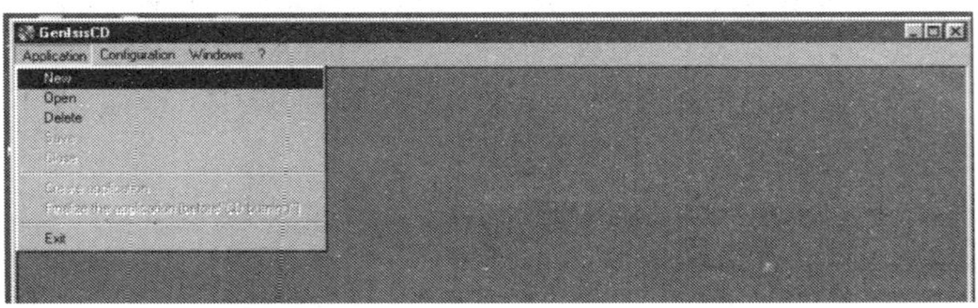


**Figure 8.10**

Then the following screen will appear.

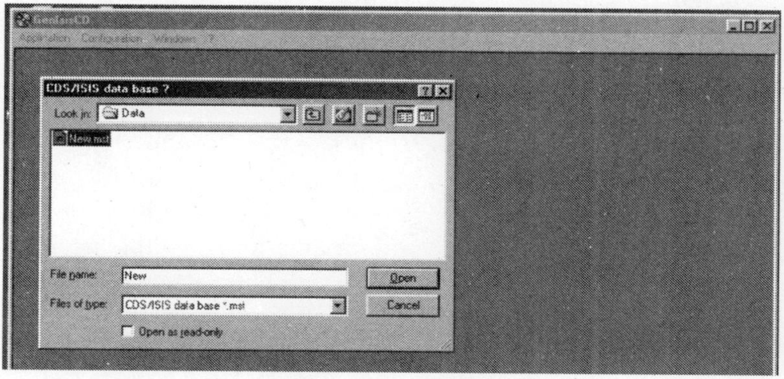


**Figure 8.11**

Select the **.mst** file of the modified WINISIS database and click **'Open'** button in the above screen. Then we will get the following screen.

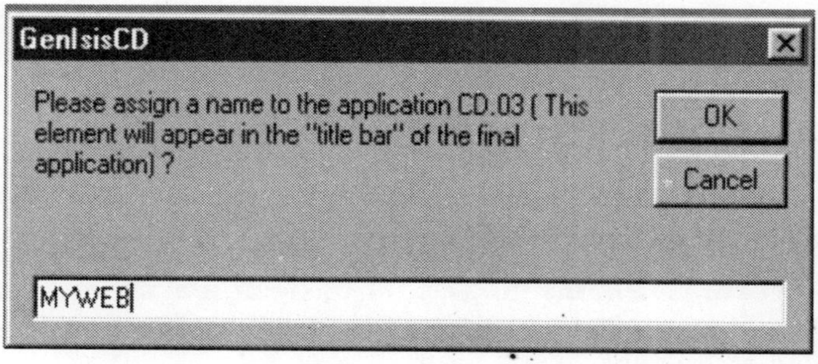


**Figure 8.12**

Give a name like **MYWEB** for our application and click **OK**.

Then we will get three window forms one over the other: **Query form**, **Format 'listing'** and **Format 'details'**

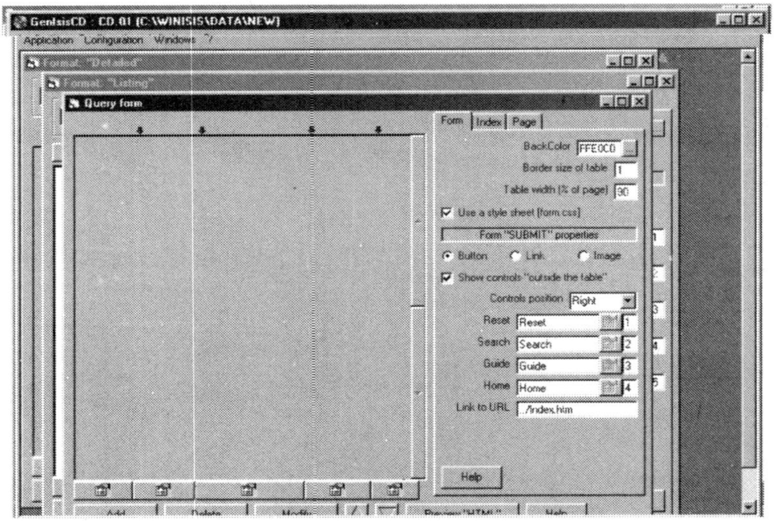

**Figure 8.13**

The form formats are

- Query form
- Format 'listing'
- Format 'details'

**Query form** allows us to design the web like *Query Form* - a front end form for searching the database.

**Format 'listing'** allows us to design a *short display format*. If we don't design a format, the default format will appear automatically.

**Format 'details'** In GenISISCD, format 'details' is not organically linked with format 'listing' and hence it has not been used in this part of the manual. We can provide detailed display with *format 'listing'*.

**How to design the query form?**

**Query Form is** the front-end web form for search by users as if in a website. It has a search box, submit button and other buttons.

To design the query form, select the **Query form** by clicking on the top of it.

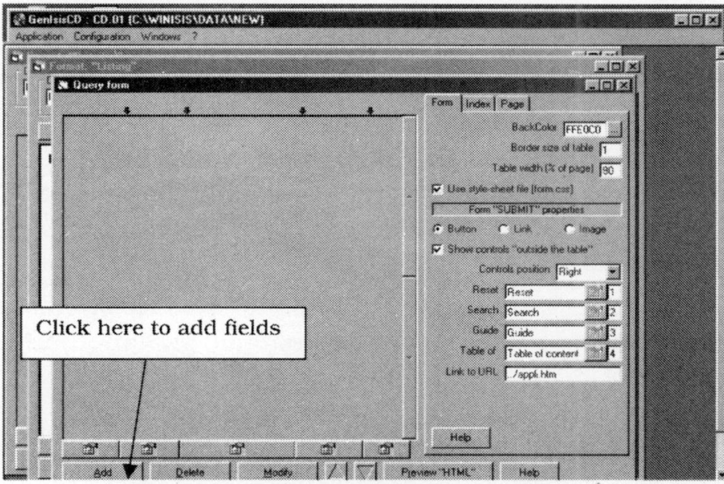


**Figure 8.14: Adding field/s to Query Form**

Then Click on **Add** button at the bottom of the query form in Figure 8.14. When we click on **Add** button we will get the following window.

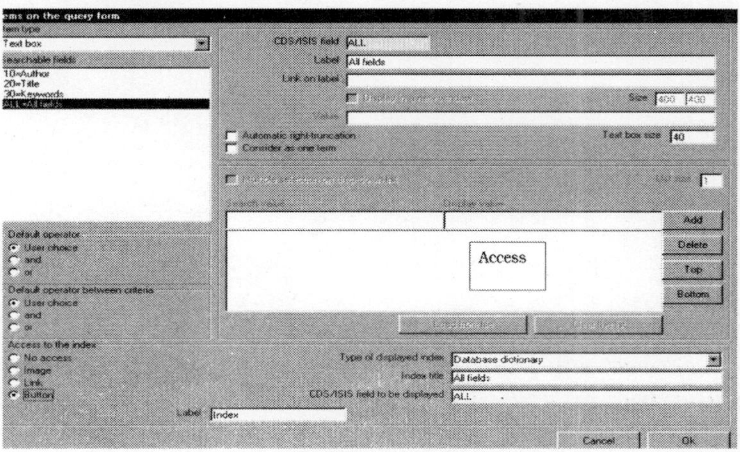


**Figure 8.15**

In the above screen, it is preferable to select **'All fields'** from the left panel (as it allows search by any term in the inverted file index of the database) and then click **Ok**

The items appearing on the left panel are the fields included in the WINISIS database. Select one field each at a time so as to have search box for all those fields in the Query form.

More fields can be included in the search box by clicking on "**Add**" button and clicking on **Ok** button. We can continue with one by one, until we select all fields and create search boxes for all fields.

From this format, we can create **search operators** check box and **index button** by marking the appropriate check box.

Then we will be lead to the following window.

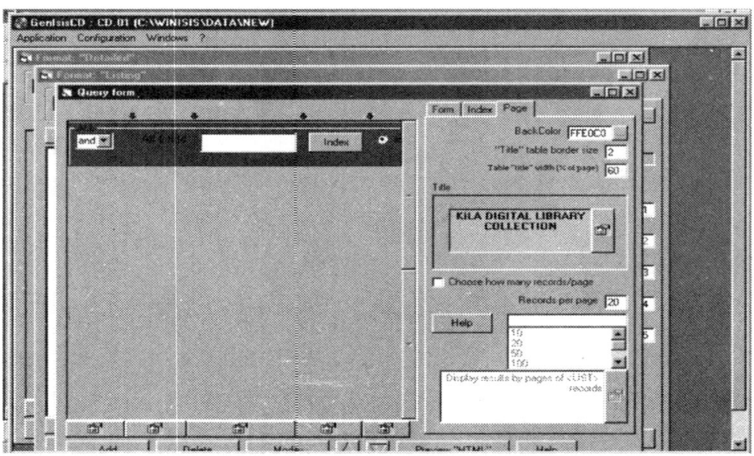


**Figure 8.16: Design Query Form**

Select any or all the three tabs **Form**, **Index** and **Page** appearing on the right side of the above screen for appropriately choosing the 'look' of the *Query Form*, *Index Display Page* and *Search Display Page*.

We can play with these options and choose anything we prefer to have a beautiful look for our cd-rom library. (For instructions to design a query form **See** *chapter 2 figure.2.28*)

**Designing format 'listing'**

Click on the *'Format-listing'* window and you will get the following default form. If we don't **Add** any field, the default search page will appear.

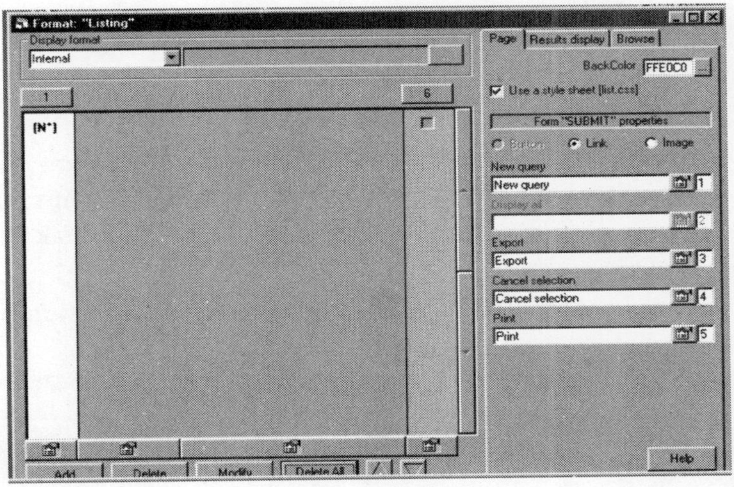


**Figure 8.17: Format 'listing' Window**

Click **Add** button at the bottom to create a customized search-result page and we will get the following window.

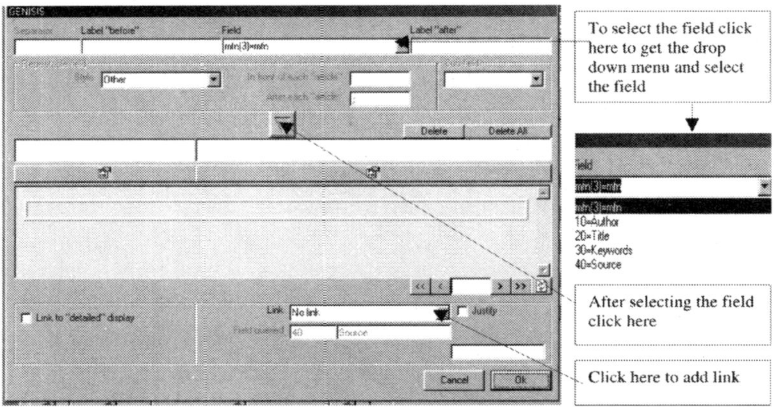


**Figure 8.18**

From the screen shown in Figure 8.18, select the appropriate **Field** in the drop down menu and then click the **down arrow** button at the middle and then click the **Ok** button.

Then select the next *field* by clicking **Add** button till all **Fields** except **Fulltext** are selected.

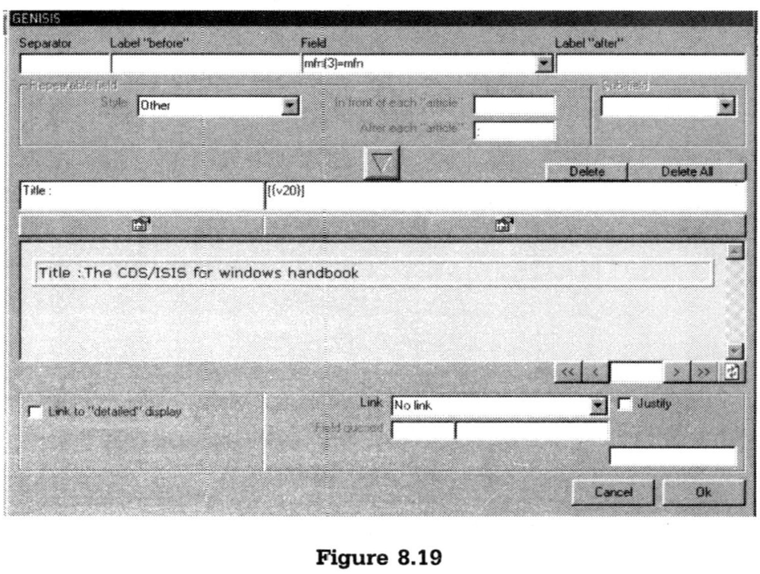


**Figure 8.19**

Select the **Fulltext** field that gives the file name (ram.pdf) of the full text document as follows.

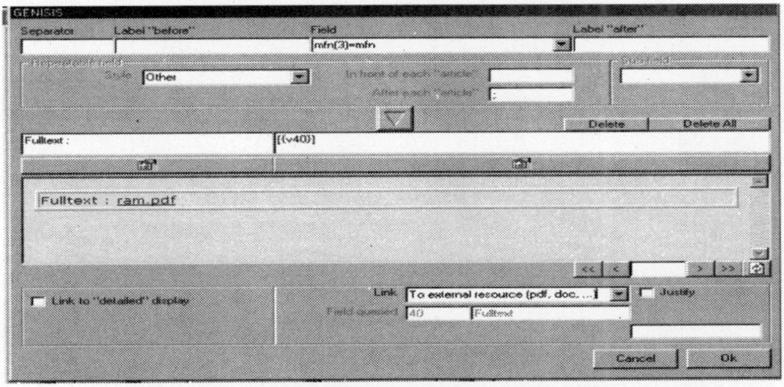

**Figure 8.20: Linking Fulltext Field to the Documents**

Then click on the **down arrow** button at the middle as above so as to display the **Fulltext** file name *ram.pdf.*

Now we can select the drop down menu appearing against **link** and select **To external resource (pdf, doc...)**, if the full text documents are pdf, doc, html etc. Then we can click **Ok** button to save it.

Then we can move on to the next screen in Figure 8.21

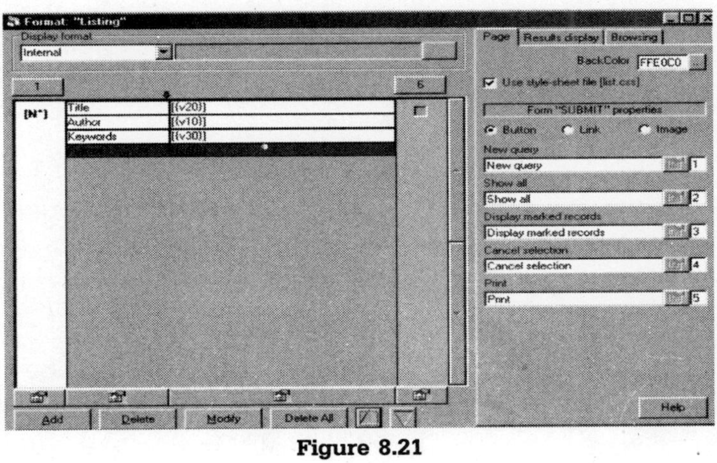

**Figure 8.21**

After designing two forms (Query form & format 'listing') as above, we may click on **Application** drop down menu and select **Create application** in figure 8.22

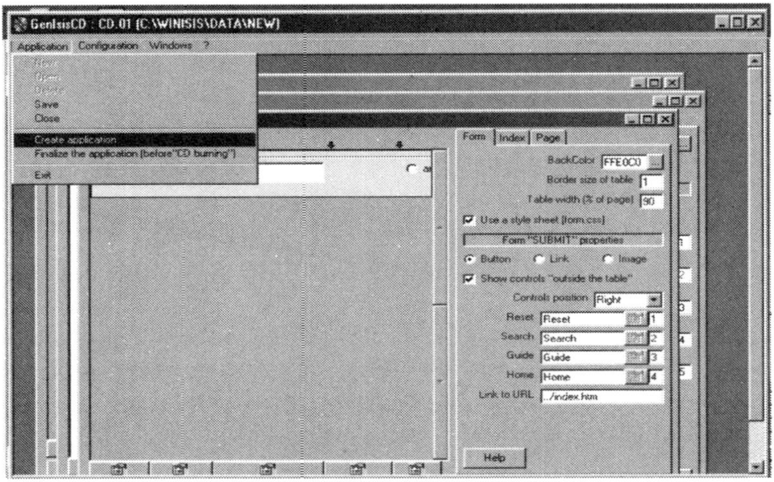


**Figure 8.22: Creating Application**

On clicking **Create application,** we will get the following screen as in Figure 8.23

**Figure 8.23**

Click the **OK** button.

Now our application would be created in the folder *C:\Program Files\GenISISCD\appli\Cd.01.*

(The second application will have the name Cd.02, third one will have Cd.03 and so on)

**Modification of files to be made before burning the cd-rom**

Open the **html** folder (C:\Program

Files\GenISISCD\appli\Cd.01\html] and Delete the **index** file

Then open the **base_databasename_01** (eg.*new.01*) folder (C:\Program Files\GenISISCD\ appli\Cd.01\ html\ base_databasename_01)

Copy **form_databasename** *(form_new)* file and paste it in the *html* folder. Then convert the name of **form_ databasename** file in html folder into **index.**

Create a *new* subfolder (say **pdf**) in the "**html**" directory. Then *copy* the set of our full text documents to the **pdf** subfolder (C:\Program Files\ GenISISCD\appli\ Cd.01\html\pdf).

Enable the resultant cd-rom to work in a computer with any cd-rom drive letter

Open the ***liste*_databasename** html file in the ***base_databasename*** folder (C:\ProgramFiles\GenISISCD\ appli\Cd.01\html\base_databasename \liste_database name) and it will look as in Figure 8.24.

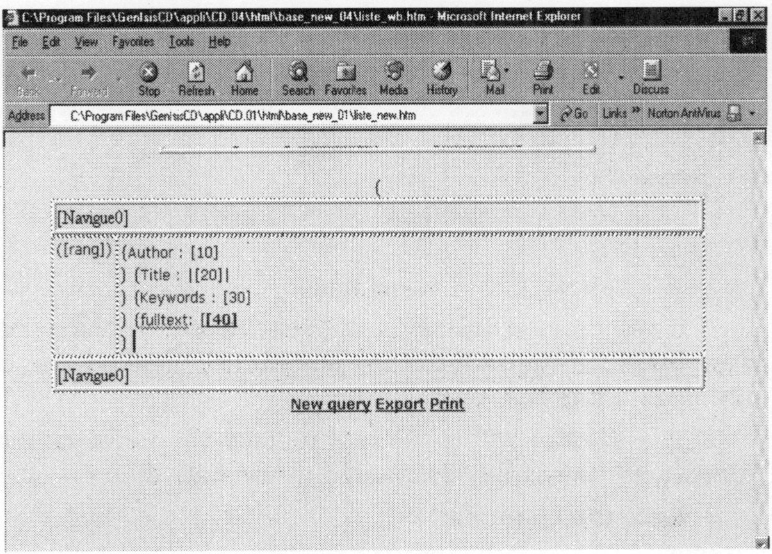


**Figure 8.24**

Then ***right click*** on the page with the mouse and select ***View sources*** to see the html code of the page. Then **html codes** will appear in a notepad file as in figure 8.25.

Now, we have to find out the *html source* pertaining to the field tag, which provides link to the full text documents (in the sample database *40 is the field tag*).

The html source line can be found out easily by searching for the * using the **Search** function of notepad.

Then add the words **[Rep]pdf/** in front of the * mark coming just before the field tag number and the resultant line would look as follows as in Figure 8.25

{<a target="_blank" href="**[Rep]pdf/***">[40]</A></B></font><BR>}

**Figure 8.25**

If we provide this syntax **[Rep]**, it will replace the letter of the cd-rom drive of the computer where cd-rom is put, even if it is D, E or F.

The symbol **"*"** (star) will replace the name of the full text document file mentioned in the field 40.

**Save** the changes

Then burn the contents in the folder **cd.01** (C:\Program Files\GenISISCD\appli\Cd.01) on a blank cd-rom.

Now we can test the cd-rom in another computer.

**Finalize the CDROM application**

Click on **Application** drop down menu and select **Finalize the application (before CD burning)** as in figure 8.26

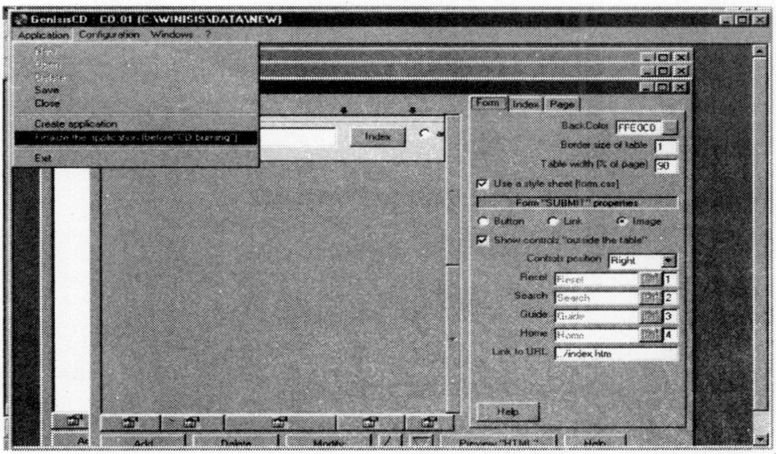

**Figure 8.26**

Then we will be lead to the following screen.

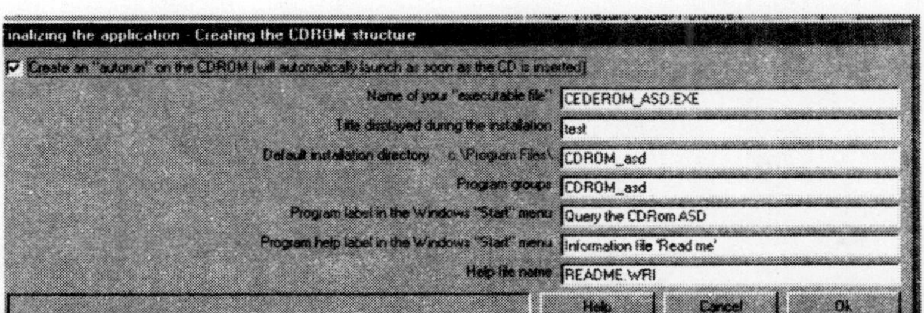


**Figure 8.27**

We may put a tick mark on the check box so as to get the *auto run* feature for the resultant cd-rom.

Then click **Ok** button in the above screen (8.27) in order to get the following screen.

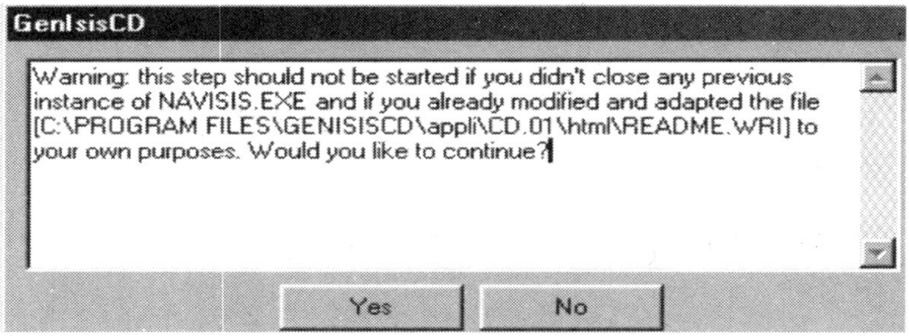


**Figure 8.28**

Click **Yes** in the above screen (8.28) to get the following screen

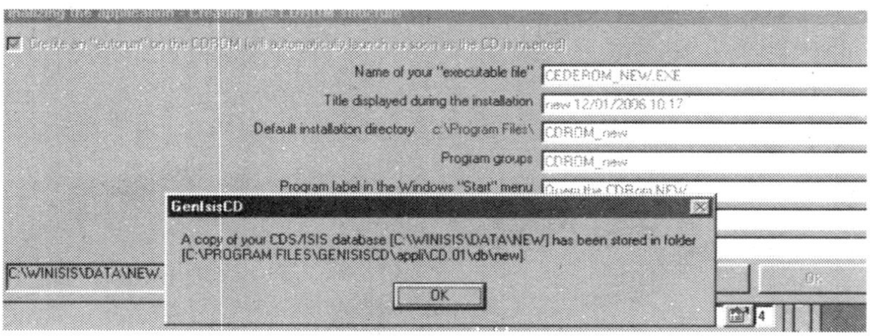


**Figure 8.29**

Click **OK** button in the screen shown in Figure 8.29.

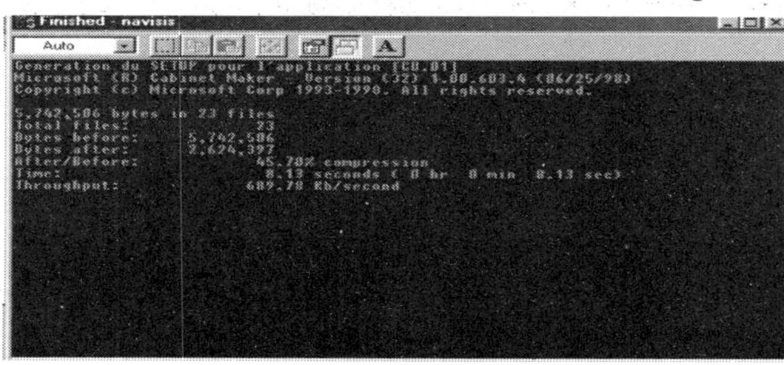


**Figure 8.30**

Allow the above screen to run till its end until it is finished.

Now click the **Close button (x)** to close the program and to get the following screen.

The screen as shown in Figure 8.31 will give the steps in burning the cd-rom.

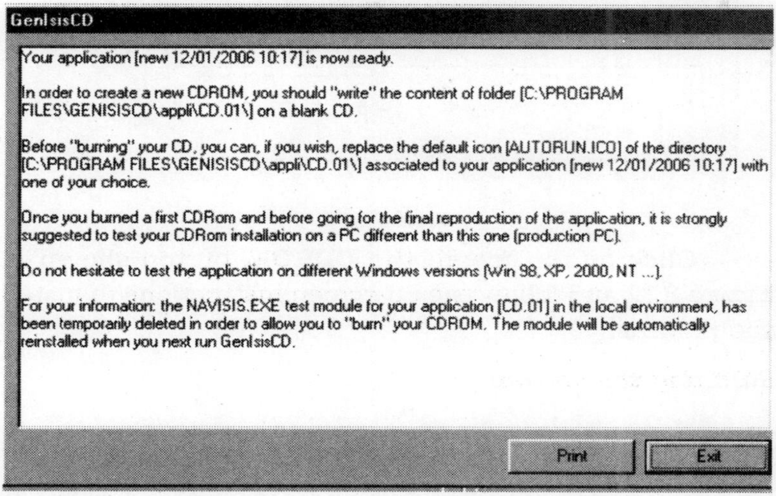


**Figure 8.31**

Click **Exit** to close the above window and to close your cd-rom file generation process.

## Testing the burned cd-rom

### *Installing the cd-rom*

Put the burnt cd-rom in any computer and the following screen will appear automatically.

If the autorun feature doesn't work, **open** the cd-rom drive to get the following screen.

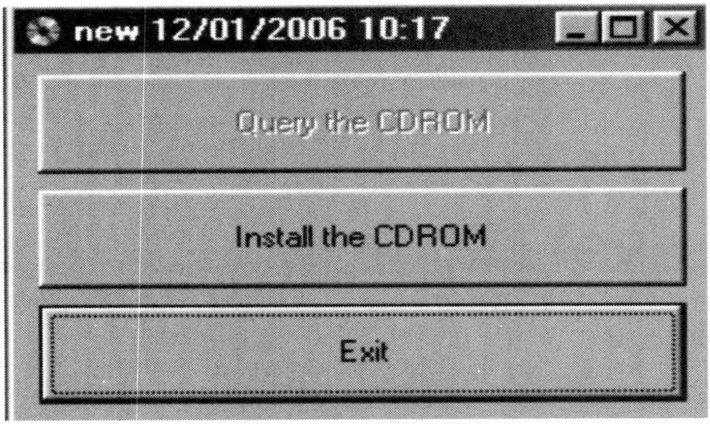


**Figure 8.32**

Click on the **Install the CDROM** button shown in Figure 8.32 and follow the on-screen instructions to install the program.

***Running the cd-rom***

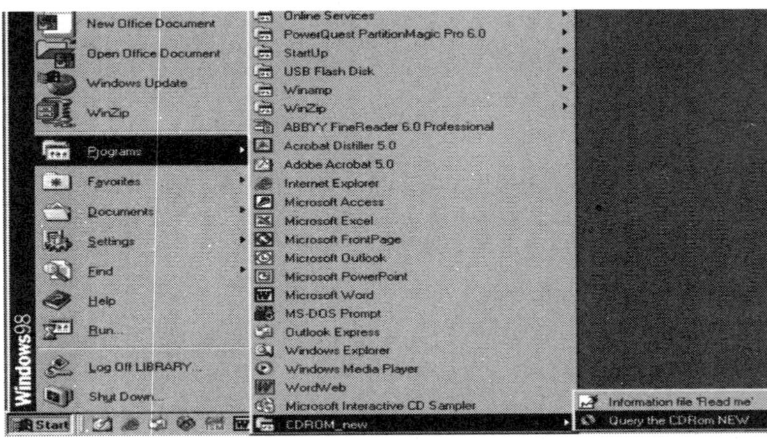


**Figure 8.33**

Then go to **Start/programs/cdrom_*name*/query the cdrom name** to open the query form as follows

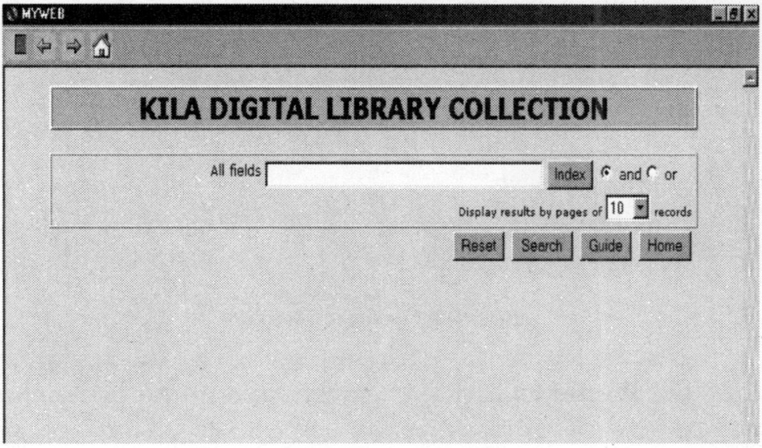


**Figure 8.34: Search Page of GenISIS CD**

Type any search term in the **search box** for all fields to make a search.

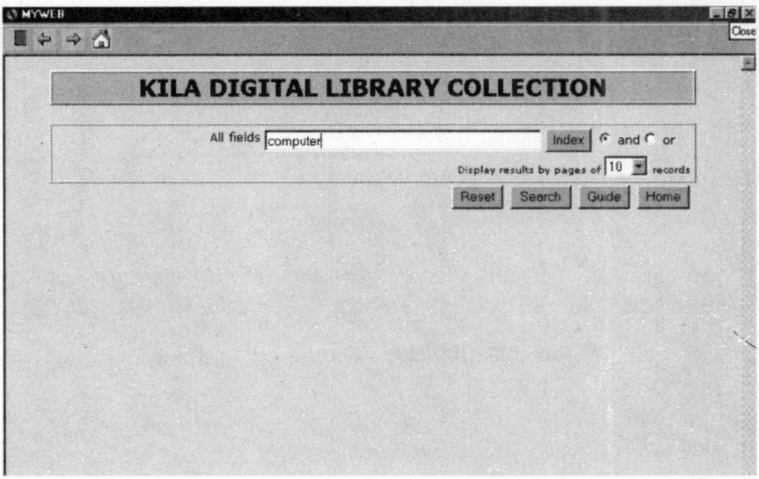


**Figure 8.35: Search Window**

Click **Search** button to get the screen as in Figure 8.36 containing the result.

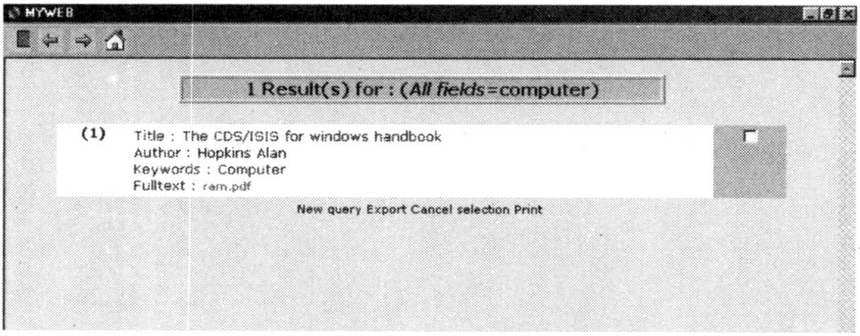


**Figure 8.36: Search Result**

If we click on the link (*ram.pdf*) appearing against the field **Fulltext** provided above, appropriate document will be opened, automatically.

**Figure 8.37: Fulltext Document Opened**

# 9 GREENSTONE

Greenstone is a suite of software for building and distributing digital library collections. It provides a new way of organizing information and publishing it on the Internet or in CD-ROM. Greenstone is produced by the New Zealand Digital Library Project at the University of Waikato, and developed and distributed in cooperation with UNESCO and the Human Info NGO. It is open-source, multilingual software, issued under the terms of the GNU General Public License. This Chapter will cover:

Software Installation
Starting New Collection
Formatting
Collection building
Customizing Appearance
CD Publication

# GREENSTONE

## BUILDING GREENSTONE DIGITAL LIBRARY

This Chapter describes the most essential steps in building up a digital library with Greenstone using very easy method.

The *Greenstone Digital Library Software* (*GSDL*) offers exciting ways to build and distribute digital document collections. It helps us to publish digital collections on the Internet or in CD-ROM. Within a few minutes time, one can build full-text *search indexes* and *browsing classifiers* for any collection of digital documents. Once initiated, the automatic collection building process may continue for several hours or days for a very large collection.

### Software Download

*Java2 Runtime Environment* can be downloaded from *http://java.sun.com/*

The *GSDL 2.80* software can be downloaded from *http://www.greenstone.org/*or *http://greenstonesupport.iimk.ac.in/our_mission.htm.*

*ImageMagick* can be had from *http://www.imagemagick.org/*

*Ghostscript* can be obtained from *http://www.cs.wisc.edu/~ghost/*

### Installation of Software

Install **Java2 Runtime Environment** in your computer as a pre-requisite for installing GSDL software. While installing the softwares, just choose the default options during the installation process.

Then install the **GSDL 2.72 (windows version)** software in your computer. Choose the Local Library mode for installation.

We may install **ImageMagick** and **Ghostscript** softwares, required to build image collections and to do advanced conversion of PDF and Postscript documents, respectively.

**Building up a Collection with *Greenstone's Librarian Interface* (GLI)**

The easiest way to build a new digital library collection is to use *GLI*, a component of Greenstone Digital Library software. GLI is a Graphical Interface program created for making the collection building process easier for librarians who do not have much knowledge to configure a collection. It works in four modes - Library Assistant, Librarian, Library System Specialist and Expert. Librarian is the suitable choice for beginner's and is the default mode. When we go up to the level of Expert, we will get more options to build. We can go to file ⇒ preference to change the mode.

GLI allows one to collect the documents, import or assign metadata, and build the documents into a digital library, and convert it into a CD-ROM library.

GLI can be used to perform the following basic activities, while building up a collection: -

1. **Gather** documents for building up the collection
2. **Enrich** the documents by adding metadata
3. **Design** the collection, its appearance and the access facilities
4. **Format** the appearance of the digital library
5. **Create** the collection
6. **Convert** the digital library into a CD-ROM library

## Start a New Collection

Open the GLI from the **Start ⇒ Programs ⇒ Greenstone Digital Library Software v2.80 ⇒ Greenstone Librarian Interface**.

To start a new collection, choose **New** from the **File** menu.

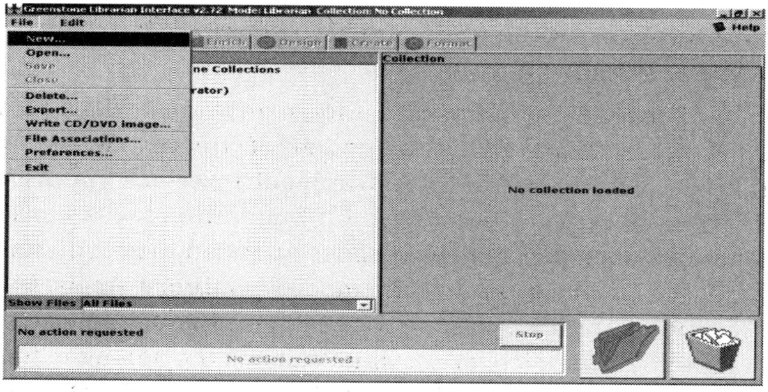


**Figure 9.1: Starting a new collection**

Fill up a name for the collection *(against Collection title)* and a brief description about the collection (against *Description of content)* in the appropriate column in the pop-up window.

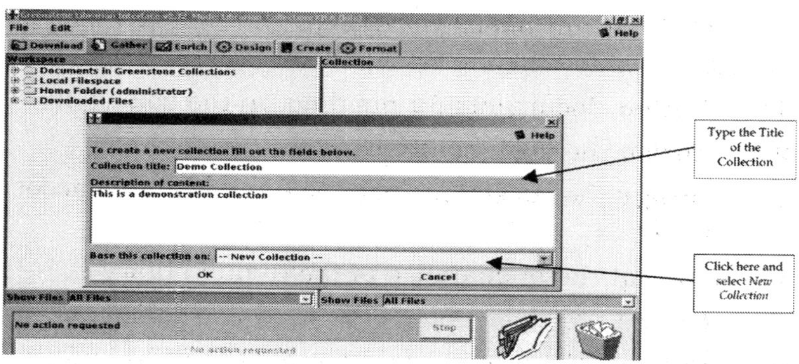


**Fig. 9.2 : Adding Information About the Collection**

Choose **New Collection** in the **Base this collection on** dialogue box and click **OK**.

This indicates that our collection to be built now will have as entirely new structure. If we want our present collection to follow the pattern of an already existing collection, select the name of that collection from the drop-down menu.

## Gather the Documents

Now the **Gather** panel will become active. Click on the required documents by exploring the entire computer. Drag and drop them into the right hand panel by our mouse. Even the entire folder with sub-folders can be dropped.

When we gather the documents, the software usually prompts you to select the Plug-in, if suitable **Plug-in** is not included. In such cases, please click the **Add Plugin** button.

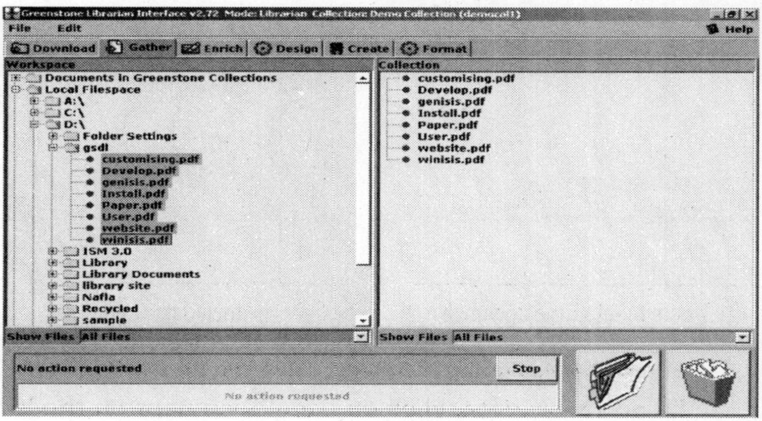


**Figure 9.3: Exploring the Computer for Gathering the Documents**

## Enriching Documents with Metadata

The next stage is to enrich the documents by adding metadata such as title, creators or subjects manually.

**Metadata** is the data about the documents, such as title, creator, subjects and so on. The metadata element pre-fixed with ***dc.*** (eg. dc.Title) which denotes dublin core metadata, ***ex.*** (eg. ex.Title) denotes extracted metadata, ***exp.*** (eg. exp.Title) denotes exploded metadata. Here we use Dublin Core metadata by giving *value* against the metadata element after selecting each document file name under *collection.*

Click on **Enrich** tab and it will bring up a panel. Left side of the panel under *Collection* tab shows the input documents. Right pane shows the *Value* box for the metadata fields.

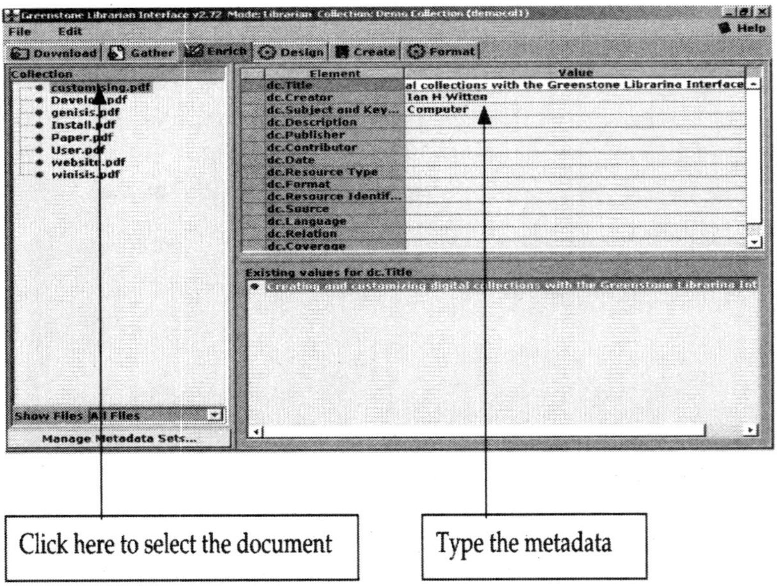


**Figure 9.4: Assigning Metadata Using the Enrich View**

To add metadata, click on each document on the left panel and type the Title of the document against **dc.Title**, type the Creator (Author) of the documents against **dc.Creator**, and type the Subjects (Keywords) against **dc.Subject and Keywords** for each selected document shown below the *Collection* tab, as in the above figure.

## Design the Collection

Then design the collection by choosing the features given under the **Design** menu. Collection design features are given in the left pane.

## Document Plug-ins

Click on **Document Plug-ins** to add the required Plug-ins needed to convert the document into the greenstone archive format.

Plug-ins, written in perl language, will translate the source document into a common form, parse them and extract metadata from them. For example, the html plug-in converts the Web pages to greenstone archive format and extract metadata that is explicit in the original document from the html source tags.

All plug-ins, needed for handling common documents, will be loaded by default at the time of installation or document *gather* process. If proper Plug-in is not loaded; the software cannot build the digital library collection.

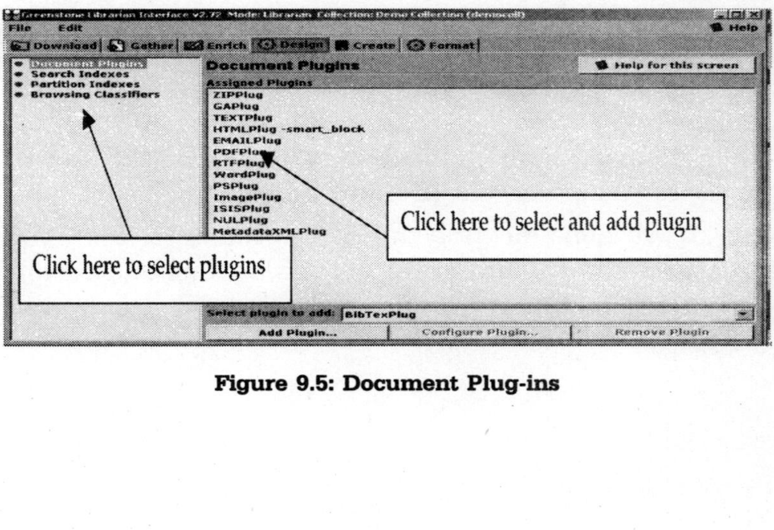


**Figure 9.5: Document Plug-ins**

## Create Search Indexes

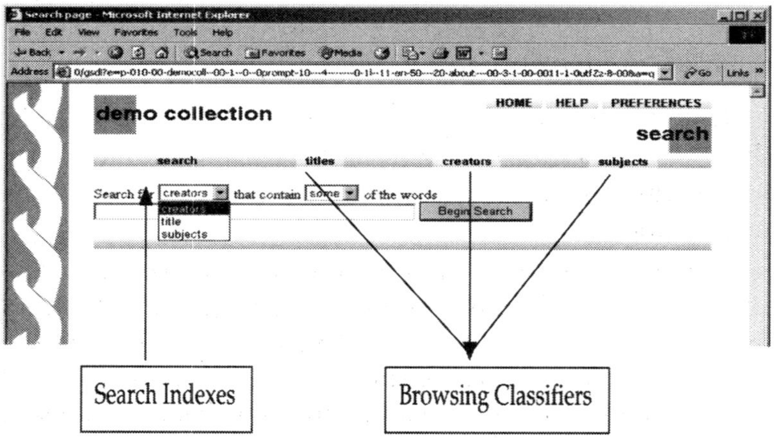


**Fig 9.6: Search Indexes and Browsing Classifiers**

Choose the **Search Indexes,** shown in Figure 9.7 on the left pane, to create *Search Indexes*.

Search Indexes determine whether to confine the search to paragraph, chapter or the entire text of the document.

## Remove Default Indexes

Remove the default indexes for *ex.Title* and *ex.Source* by selecting the index description under *Assigned Indexes* and then by clicking on the **Remove Index** button. Retain the *search index* for **text [Default Index]**.

If we don't provide the search index for text, you cannot search the entire text of the document. Make it default, preferably.

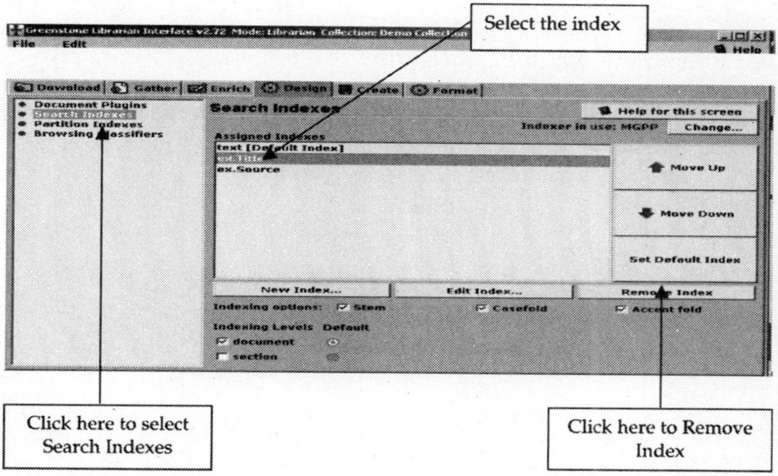


**Figure 9.7: Removing Index**

## Adding Search Indexes

Click on the **New Index** button. Select the **dc.Title**, **dc.Creator** and **dc.Subject and Keywords,** by tick marking on the check box one by one, and add them one by one by clicking on the **Add Index** button. That means, select *dc.Title* first and add it, then select *dc.Creator* and add it and so on.

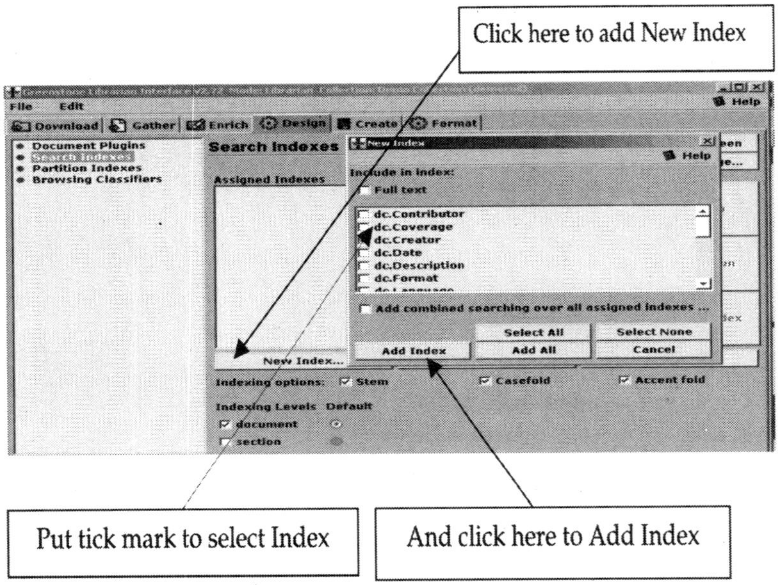


**Figure 9.8: Adding Indexes**

At the end, all the three indexes will be added one by one as in the figure 9.9.

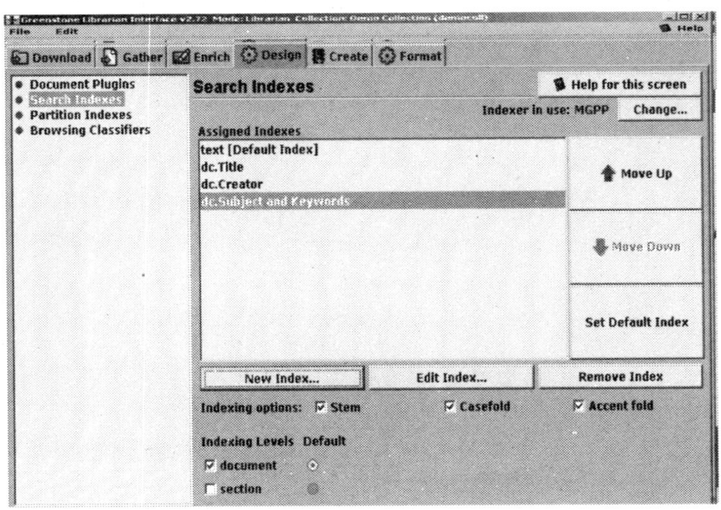


**Figure 9.9: Indexes Selected for the Collection**

We may select an index and move it up or move it down by clicking on the buttons on the right side so as to set the order of its appearance. Likewise we can set any *index* as *default index* by using the **Set Default Index** button.

### Browsing Classifiers

Browsing Classifiers such as Titles, Creators, Subjects (see the Figure 9.10) need to be created to browse the collection.

Select **Browsing Classifier** by clicking on it and then click on the **Remove classifier** button to remove the default Browsing Classifiers for **Title** and **Source** as shown in Figure 9.10.

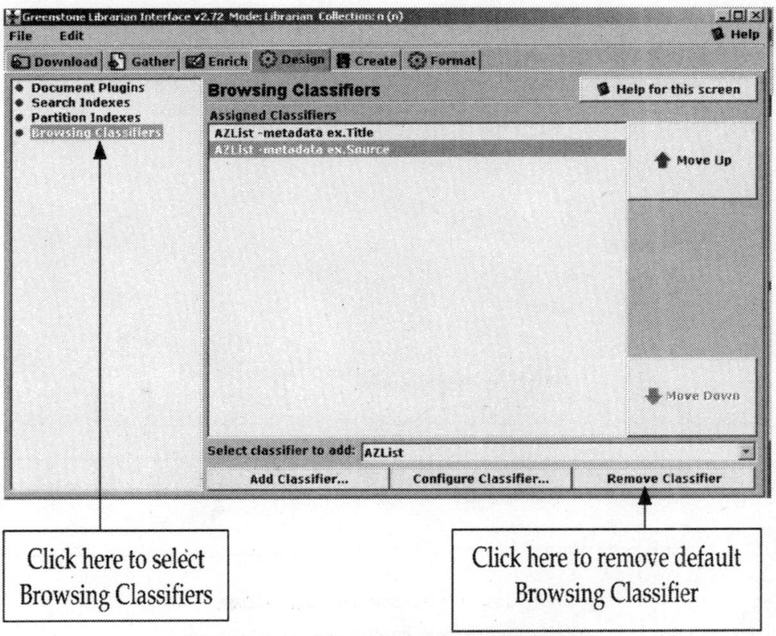


**Fig 9.10: Default Browsing Classifiers**

Now, choose **Select classifier to add** pull down list and select **A-Z List** or **A-Z Compact List**.

Use of AZCompactList Classifier brings bookshelf icons under the browsing classifier. It groups together the documents that appear multiple times with same metadata and does not differ with AZList in any other manner.

Then click on **Add Classifier** and add the Browsing Classifiers for **Title**, **Creators** and **Subjects** by one by one.

Title, Creators and Subjects are the default button names for dc.Title, dc.Creator and dc.Subject and Keywords. You can change the *button name* by marking the *button name* check box and typing the new *button name* against it, while configuring the *browsing classifiers*. It is better to use the default *button name* initially, so as to avoid the complexities.

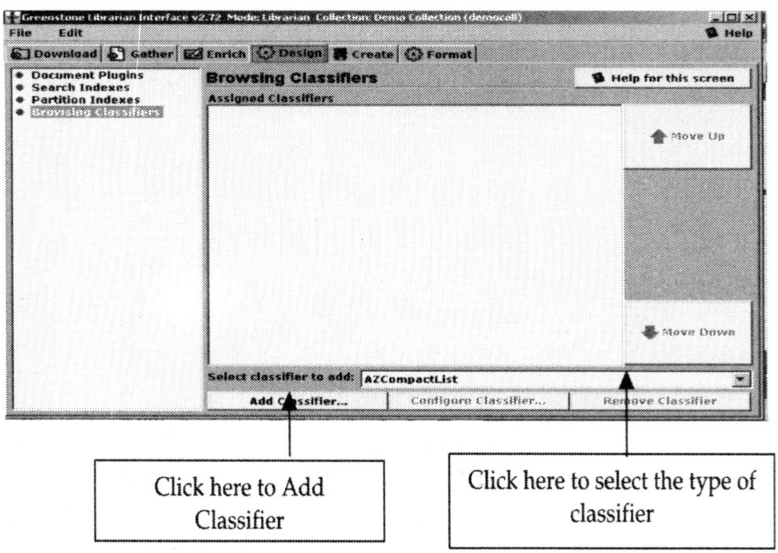


**Figure 9.11: Adding Classifier**

When we click **Add Classifier** button in the above screen, we will get the window for choosing the **Browsing Classifier**. Select the browsing classifier for *Title* by choosing the metadata *dc.Title* as follows:-

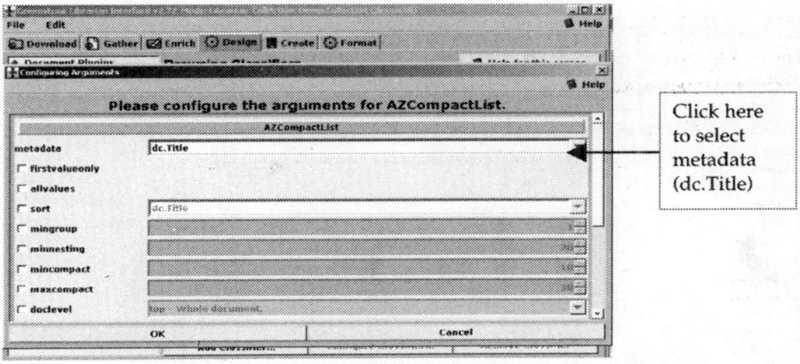


**Figure 9.12: Adding Classifier CL1 for Title - dc.Title**

Click **OK** button to add *Title* classifier.

Then select the browsing classifier for *Creator* by choosing the metadata option *dc.Creator* as follows:-

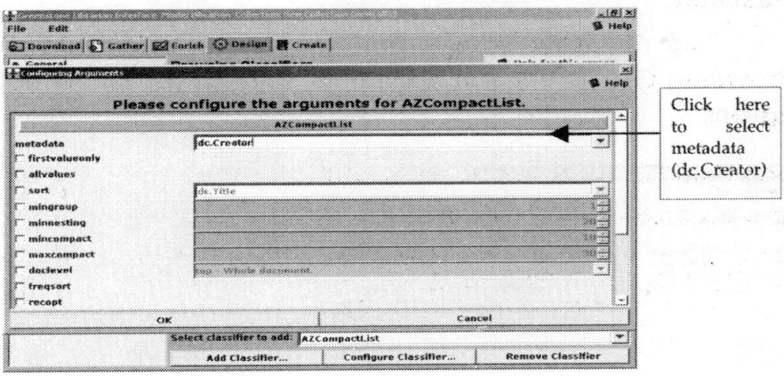


**Figure 9.13: Adding Classifier CL2 for Creator - dc.Creator**

Click **OK** button to add *Creator* classifier.

Then select the browsing classifier for *Subjects* by choosing the metadata option *dc.Subject and Keywords* as follows:-

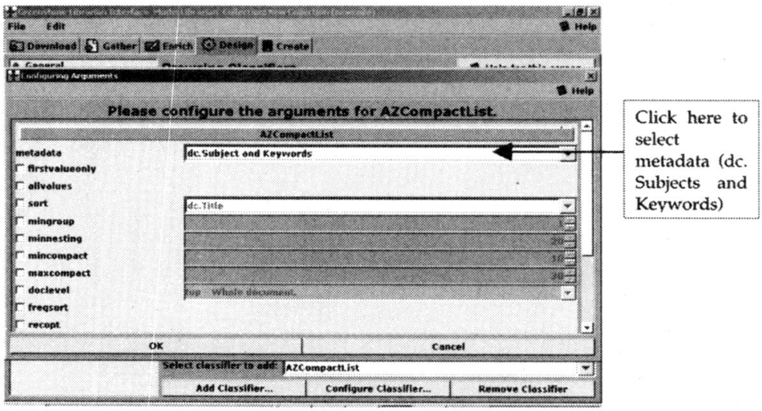


**Figure 9.14: Adding Classifier CL3 for Subjects – dc.Subject and Keywords**

Click **OK** button to add *Subject and Keywords* classifier.

The resultant screen that shows the three added Browsing Classifiers will appear as seen in the following figures

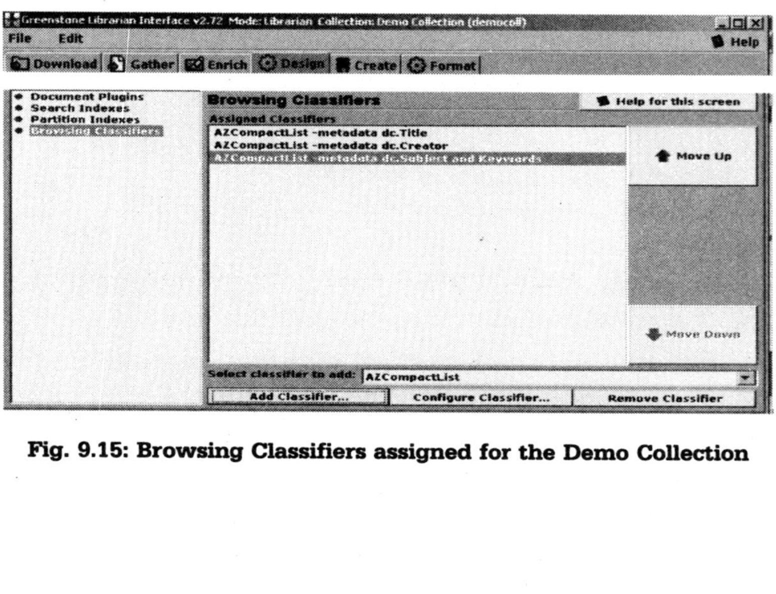


**Fig. 9.15: Browsing Classifiers assigned for the Demo Collection**

## Format

The page-display of the resultant digital library is governed by the **Format features** given below the **Format** tab.

## General

Choose the **Format** Tab and select **General** to provide the general information about the collection.

## Put a picture as a collection icon

Click on the **Browse** button on middle right, choose a small picture of around *100*100* pixels and select the picture so as to appear it as the collection icon.

The same picture or a different picture can be used as the image for the 'about page'. About page is the first page about an individual digital library collection that contains a short description about the collection.

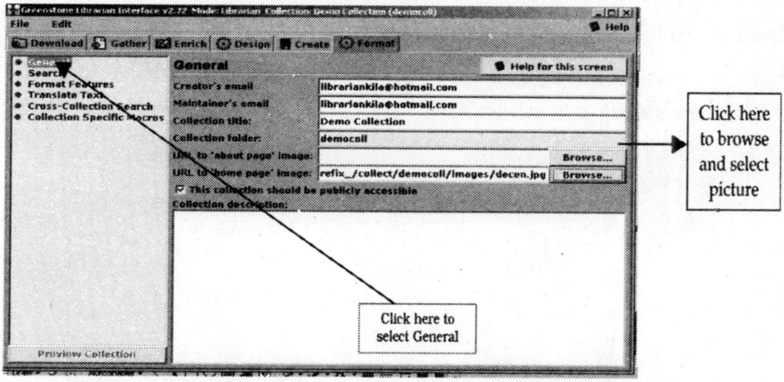


**Figure 9.16: Designing the Collection – General Information**

## Format Features

Beginner's may skip the *Format Features* section and go to the next section **(2.5 Build the collection**). If we skip, the default settings will take care of the page-display.

There are two types of Format Statements - General

statement applicable in general to all and specific statement applicable to specific classifier or search list. Specific statements, if present, would override the general statements.

Let us examine some statements

VList - applies to all vertical lists in all classifiers

Search VList - applies to all search result lists

CL2HList - applies to all hierarchy lists in classifier 2

The value of any metadata can be interpolated by placing the metadata name in square brackets. eg. [Title] in the format statements.

[link] [icon] [/ link] provides a link from icon to the HTML version of the document.

[link] [Title] [/link] provides link from the Title of the document.

[srclink] [srcicon] [/srclink] provides a link from the word/pdf icon to the word/pdf version of the document.

Advanced users can use the **Format Features** section of the **Format** panel on the left pane as follows: -

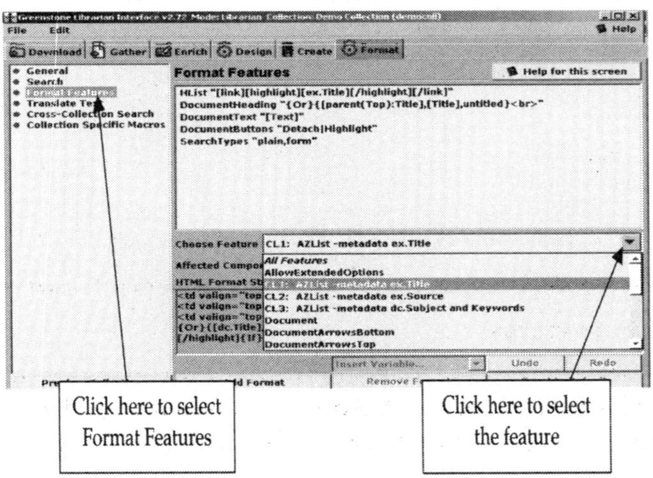


**Fig. 9.17: Modifying the Format Features**

If we want to change any format feature, select the appropriate one (eg. CL1 AZList- metadata dc.Title) from the **Choose Feature** pull down list and add the format string to the **Format Features** by clicking on the **Add Format** button. Appropriate feature can change the appearance of the digital library. Learning the format features in the beginning stage is a bit difficult. But it is not much difficult to manage. The CL1 Browsing classifier for Title can be added as shown in the screen of Figure 9.18.

CL1 denotes the first browsing classifier dc.Title and CL2 denotes the second one dc.Creator and so on.

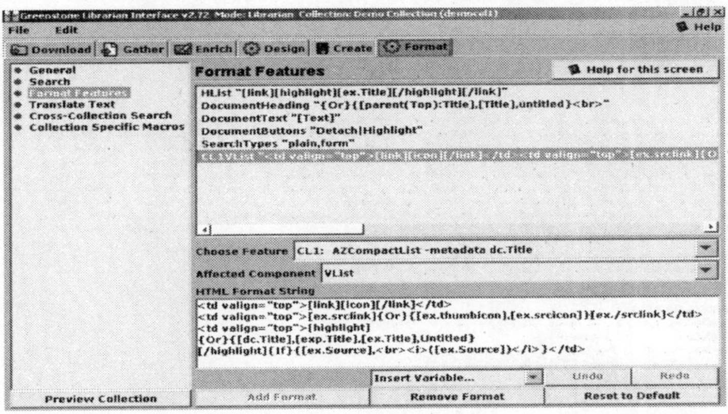

**Figure 9.18: Adding CL1 Browsing Classifier for dc.Title**

Similarly select any string from **Choose Feature** box and click **Add Format** button to edit it to change the display. The **HTML Format String** box shown below is for editing the strings.

As shown above, we can add **CL2** and **CL3** classifiers for **Creators** and **Subjects** and can make modifications if we have reasonable knowledge of HTML.

**Build the Collection**

Then go to the **Create** panel. Click on the **Build Collection** button and the progress bar will show the progress in building the collection.

During the building process, the text of the documents will be compressed and the indexes specified will be generated in order to ensure the availability of the collection for search and retrieval. *GNU Data Base Manager,* a program used within the Greenstone software, will store the metadata of each document. *Managing Gigabytes* is the program used by the Greenstone system for fulfilling indexing that incorporates compression techniques.

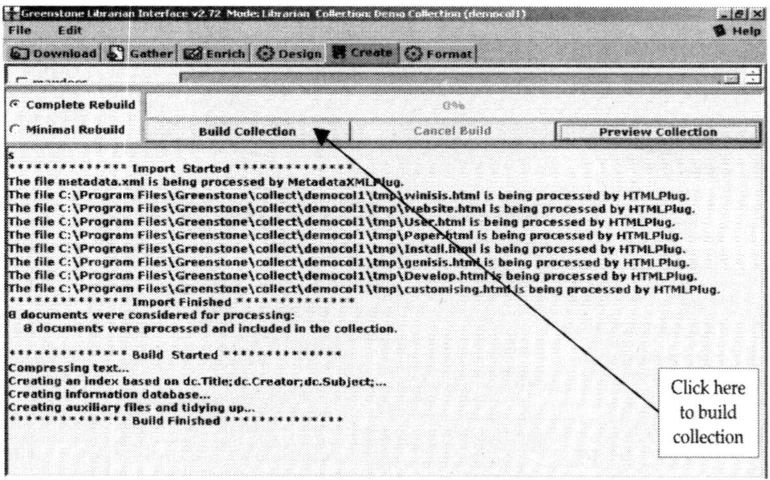


**Figure 9.19: Building a Collection**

## Preview the Collection

At the end of the building process, Click on the **Preview Collection** button to view the collection built.

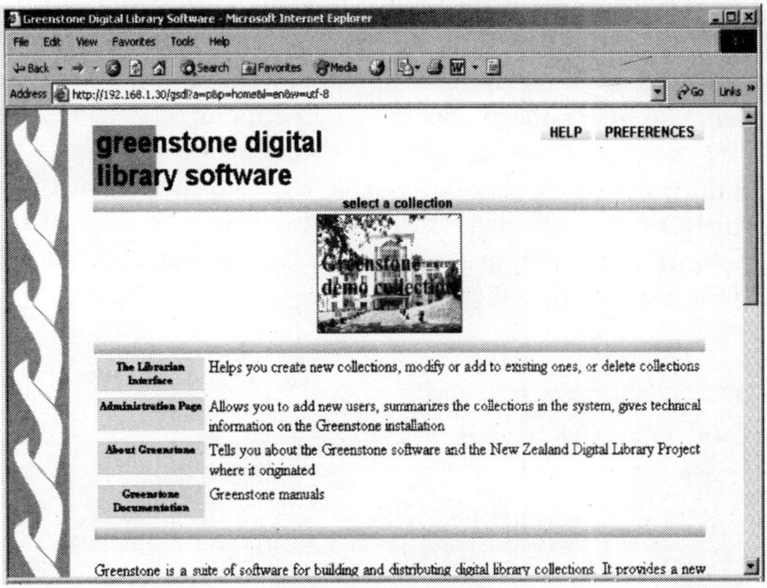


**Figure 9.20: Home Page of the Demo Collection**

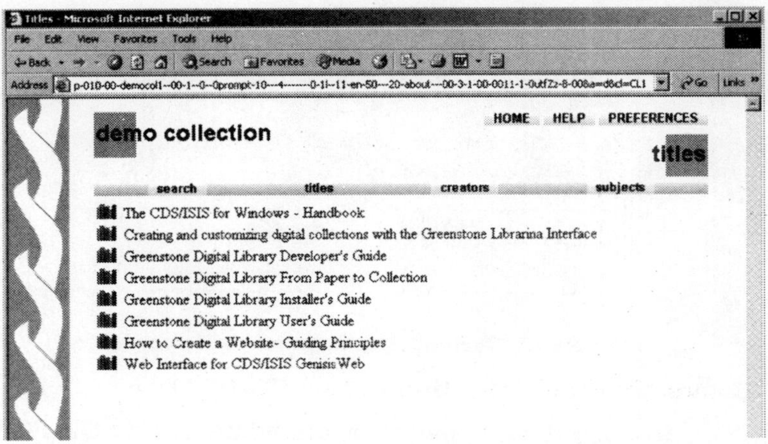


**Figure 9.21: Browse the Collection by Title Classifier**

## Customizing the Appearance of Greenstone

The easiest way to change the appearance of Greenstone home page is to modify the images such as *gsdlhead.gif, chalk.gif, bg_green.gif* appearing in the folder *C:\Program Files\Greenstone\images* suitably. The homepage is created '*on the fly*' when we run the application, by drawing up the images and other instantaneously created values. So if we change the image, the appearance will change.

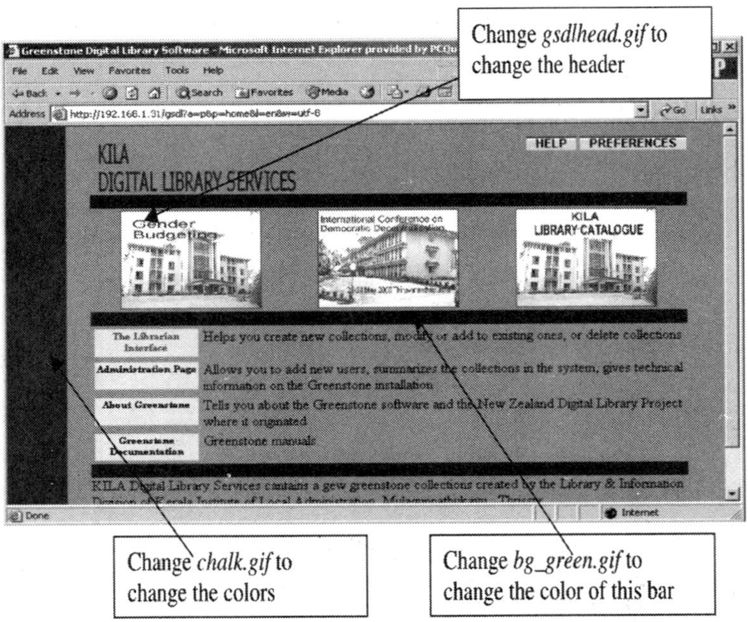


**Figure 9.22: Customizing Greenstone Homepage**

## Converting the Collection in to a CD-ROM

To convert our Greenstone application into a CD-ROM for distribution among wider audience, click on **File ⇒ Write CD/DVD image......**as follows:-

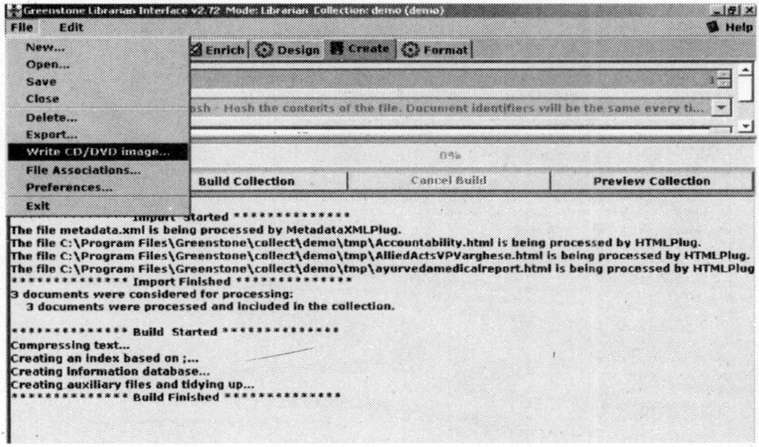


**Figure 9.23: Starting the Export Process**

A pop-up window will appear as follows:-

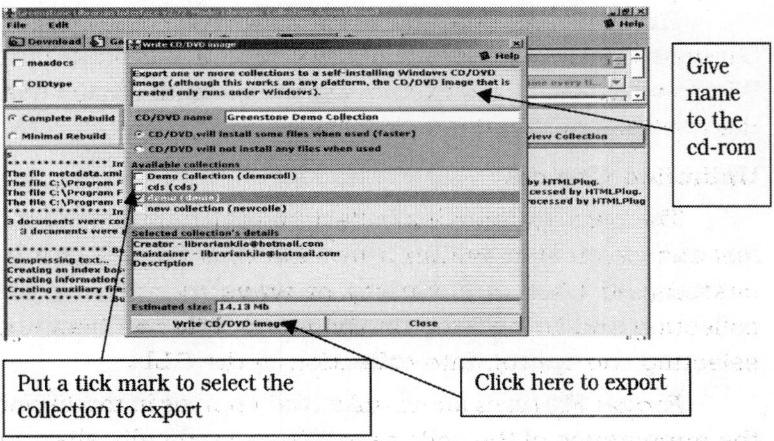


**Figure 9.24: Giving a Collection Name for CD-ROM**

Provide a name for our CD-ROM, mark the check box pertaining to the collection to be exported and click ***Write CD/DVD image*** button.

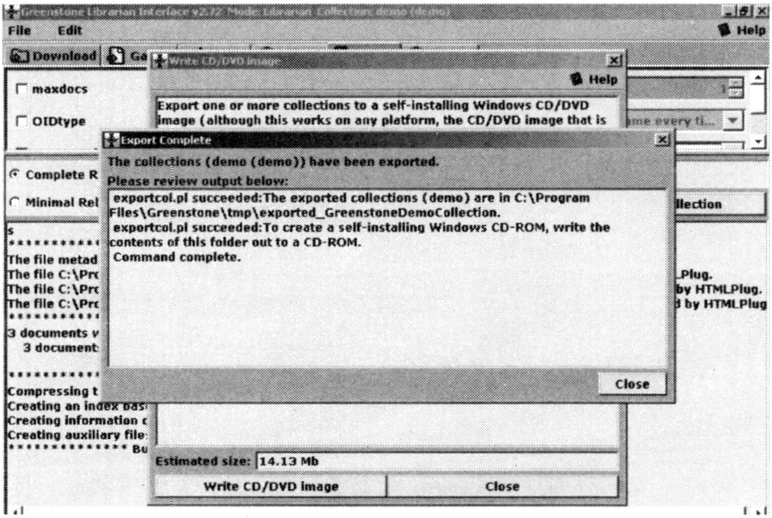

**Figure 9.25: Export completed**

Click **Close** button.

Then burn the contents of the folder (C:\ProgramFiles\Greenstone\tmp\exported_Demo) into a self-installing Windows CD-ROM after removing the *gsdlsite.cfg* file from the contents of the above said folder.

**Unlimited Choices**

The basic greenstone collection with normal *look and feel* can be created within a few minutes time. It can be customized later in a variety of ways by opening the collection and by clicking on the menu, **File ⇒ Open** and selecting the appropriate collection in the GLI .

*Format Features* allow unlimited choices in modifying the appearance of the collection. We can radically alter the style of the pages generated, by changing the *macro* files included in the 'macro' folder of the Greenstone installation.

Greenstone can be used fruitfully for managing digital knowledge resources.

# 10

# WINISIS-GREENSTONE CONVERSION

Greenstone package promoted by UNESCO is used by numerous institutions to web-host their digital libraries and institutional repositories. This chapter discusses how a WINISIS archive can be converted into a Greenstone Digital Library for hosting in the Web. This chapter will cover.

- Gathering the Data Format
- Exploding Meta Database
- Collection Design
- Formatting
- Collection Building

# WINISIS-GREENSTONE CONVERSION

## WINISIS TO GREENSTONE CONVERSION

Converting an WINISIS Archive into a Greenstone Digital Library

WINISIS archive with full text document can be converted into greenstone collection easily. For that we have to create a WINISIS archive as follows:-

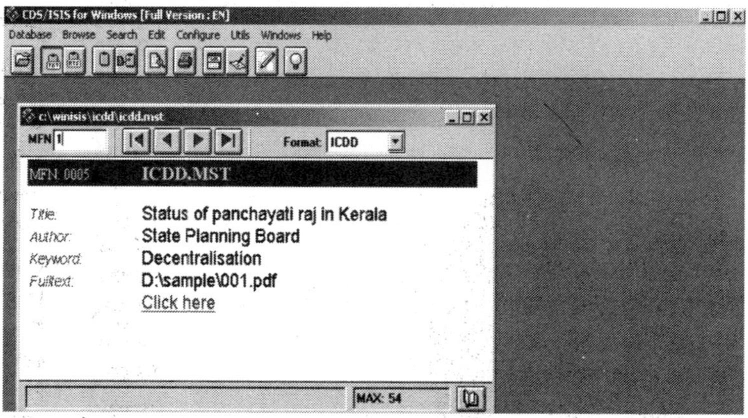


**Figure 10.1: WINISIS Archive of Digital Documents**

### Creating the Collection with Greenstone

Open the Greenstone Librarian Interface (GLI) **Start ⇒ Programs ⇒ Greenstone Digital Library Software v2.72 ⇒ Greenstone Librarian Interface.**

To create a new collection, choose **New** from **File** menu

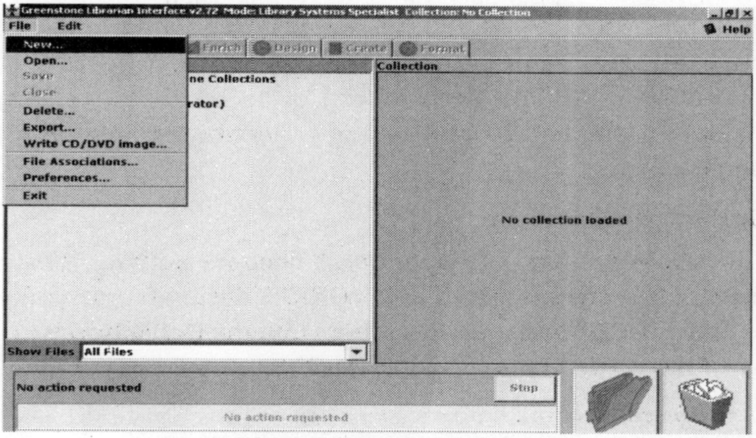


**Figure 10.2: Starting a New Collection**

Give a title for the collection (say **WINISIS**) and give a short description about the collection as shown in the Figure 10.3.

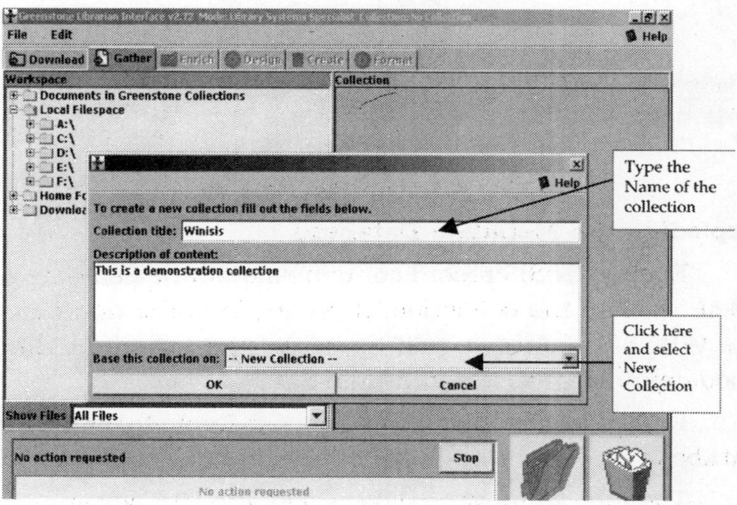


**Figure 10.3: Collection Name and Description**

Choose **New Collection** in the **Base this collection on** dialogue box and click **OK.**

This indicates that our collection to be built now will have entirely new structure. If we want our present collection to follow the pattern of an already existing collection, select the name of that collection from the drop-down menu.

## Gather the Database

Now the **Gather** panel will become active. Locate **.mst, .fdt & .xrf** files from your WINISIS database (normally at *C:\WINISIS\data*) and drag them into the **Collection** pane as in the screen shown in Figure 10.5.

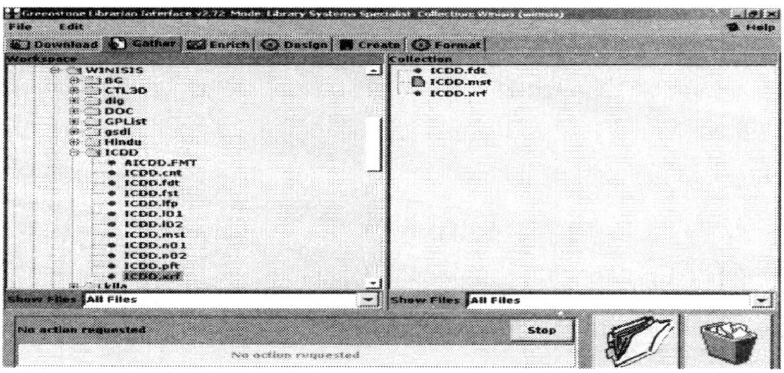


**Figure 10.4: Gathering the Files**

## Exploding the Metadata Database

Each WINISIS record contains metadata elements of documents in the collection. If we explode the database, the WINISIS database will be converted into individual documents with associated metadata.

Right click the **.mst** file and choose **Explode metadata database**.

Then the window as shown in Figure 10.6 will appear. Provide explode parameters as in Figure 10.6.

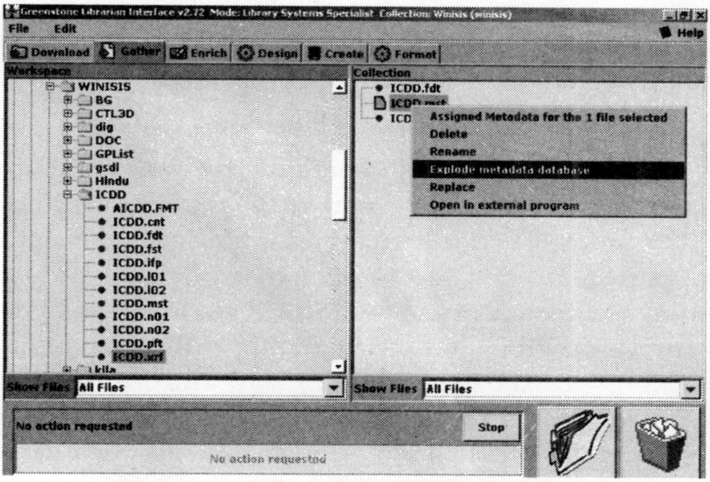


**Figure 10. 5: Explode Metadata Database**

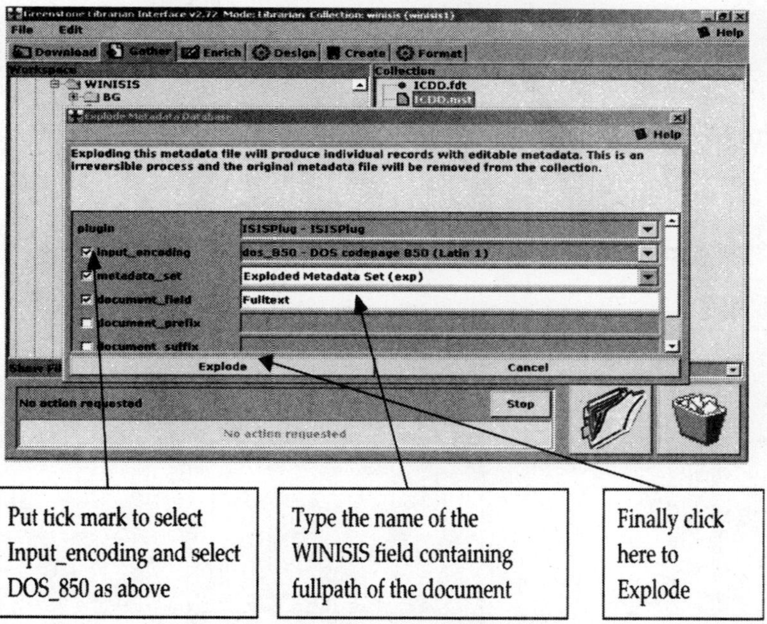


**Figure 10.6: Explode Parameters**

In the screen shown in Figure 10.6 select:-

**Input_encoding** - dos_850-DOS codepage 850 (Latin 1)

**document_field** - Full text (it provide the *field name* in WINISIS that holds the full path **document_prefix** –leave it as blank

**document_suffix** - leave it as blank

If the document field contains the document name (eg.ram) alone, provide the part of the path to be prefixed (eg. D:\sample\) in document_prefix and the file extension (eg. .pdf) in the document suffix. If we don't provide full path of the document in the WINISIS database field, it is better to provide document name with extension in document_suffix (eg.ram.pdf) and the folder name (eg.D:\sample\) in the doument_prefix. Whatever be, the full path of the document location should be concatenated from document_field, document_prefix and document_suffix (eg. D:\sample\ram.pdf)

Then click on **Explode** and click on **Ok** when explode is completed.

**View the files in the Enrich Panel**

We can view the full text documents in the **Enrich** panel as in Figure 10.7.

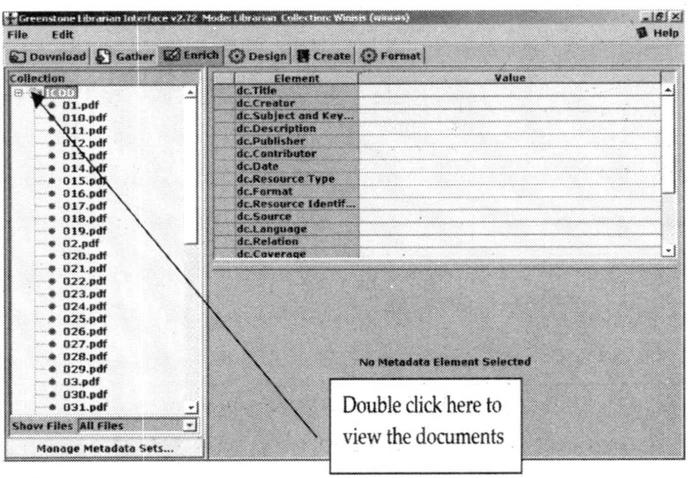


**Figure 10.7: View the Documents**

If the documents in the **Collection** pane of **Enrich** panel appears as dummy files with **nul** extension (.nul), the files are not gathered and something has gone wrong in collection building. So ensure that the **Collection** pane shows the exact documents file name with extension (eg. 01.pdf).

**Enrich** panel is meant for adding /viewing metadata. You can view the metadata of each document by clicking on it in the left pane.

The metadata elements with prefix **exp.** (exp.Title, exp.Author etc.) are only when you explode the database. The Dublin Core Metadata such as dc.Title, dc.Creator etc. are of no consequence.

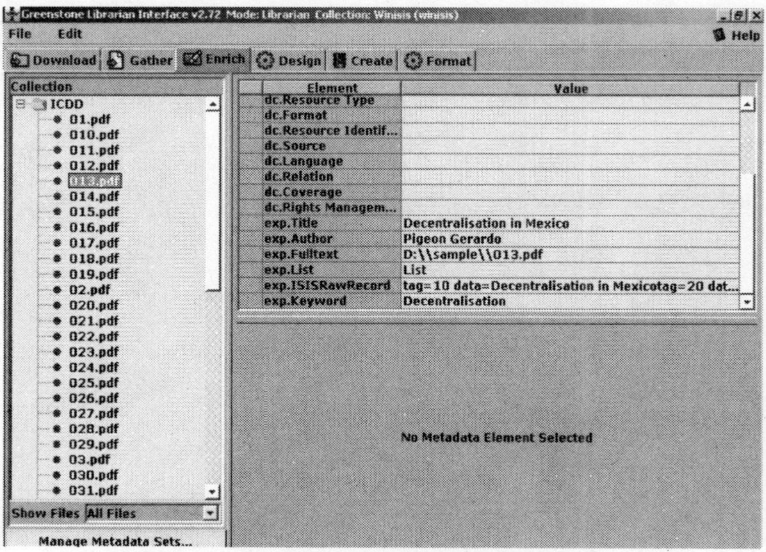


**Figure 10.8: Metadata set of each document**

## Designing the Collection

Then design the collection by choosing the following features given under the **Design** menu. Collection design consists of many facets enlisted in the left pane.

## Create Search Indexes

Choose the **Search Indexes,** shown on the left pane, for creating *Search Indexes*. Search Indexes determine whether to confine the collection search to paragraph, chapter or the entire text of the document. If we need full text search, keep the *Search Index* for *Text* and retain it as default index.

## Remove the Default Indexes

Remove the default indexes for *ex.Title* and *ex.Source* by selecting the index description under *Assigned Indexes* and then by clicking on the **Remove Index** button. Do not remove the *search index* for **text [Default Index]**.

If we don't provide the *search index* for text, we cannot search the entire text of the document. Make it default, preferably.

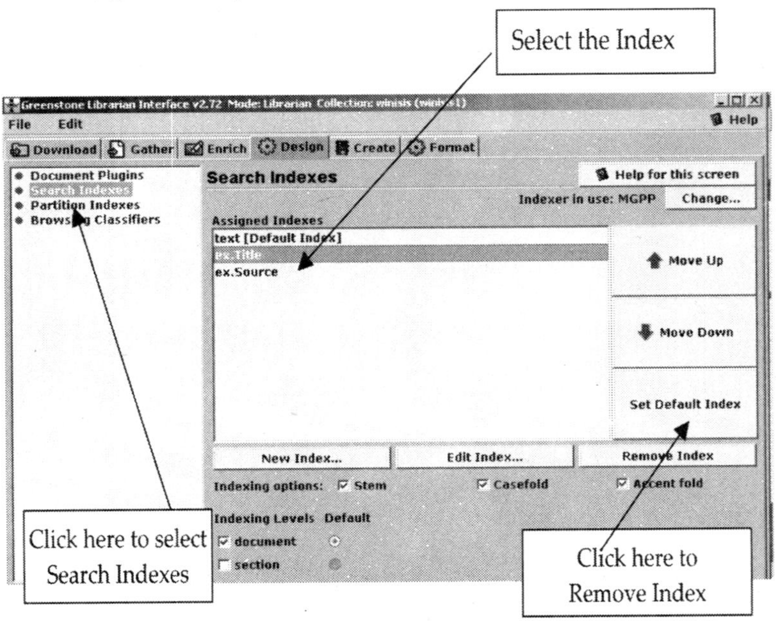


**Figure 10.9: Removing Index**

## Adding New Indexes

Click on the **New Index** button. Select the **exp.Title**, **exp.Author** and **exp.Keyword**, by tick marking on the check box one by one, and add them one by one by clicking on the **Add Index** button. That means select *exp.Title* first and add it, then select *exp.Author* and add it, then select *exp.Keyword* and so on.

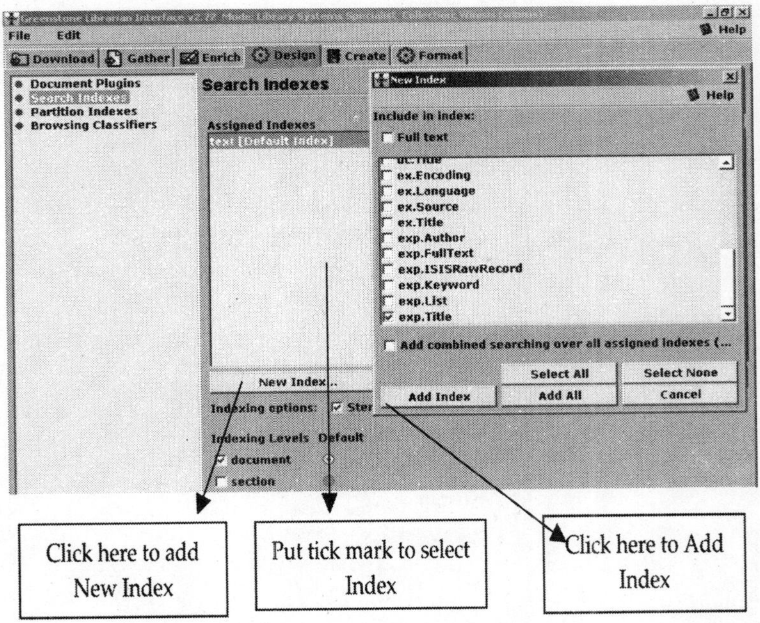


**Figure 10.10 : Adding Index for exp.Title**

Select and add the Search Index for *Author* by choosing the metadata (*exp.Author*) as follows:-

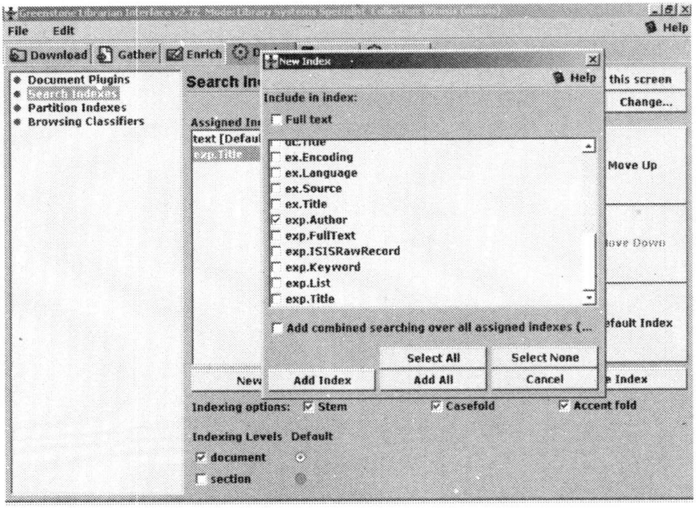

**Figure 10.11 : Search Index for exp.Author**

Select and add the Search Index for *Keyword* by choosing the metadata (*exp.Keyword*) as follows:-

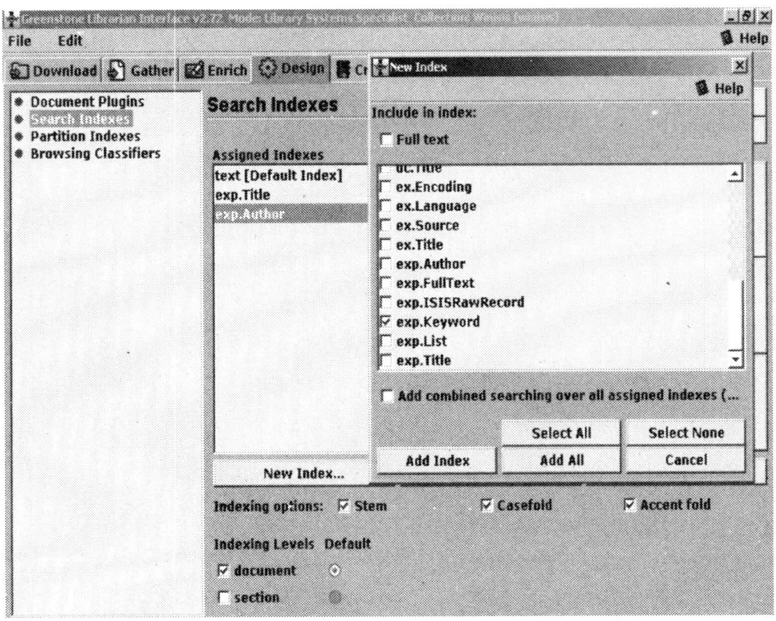

**Figure 10.12: Search Index for exp.Keyword**

At the end, all the three indexes will be added one by one as in the Figure 10.13.

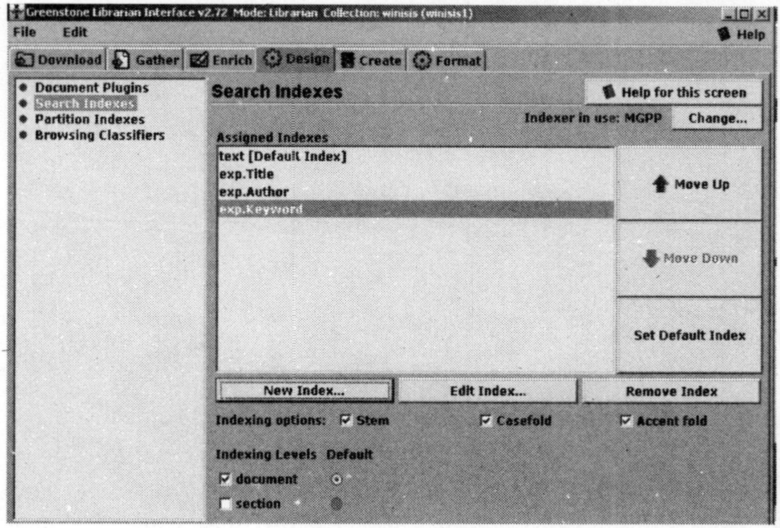


**Figure 10.13: Indexes Selected for the Collection**

We can move any index up or down to set its order of appearance by selecting the index and clicking on the buttons on the right side. Likewise we can set any *index* as *default index* by selecting the index and clicking on the **Set Default Index** button.

## Browsing Classifiers

If we want to browse on a metadata element, we must set up a Browsing Classifier, independently of creating a search index on this metadata element. The metadata used for the database are *Author, Title & Keyword* and we need to create browsing classifiers for them. The default Browsing Classifiers are as follows:-

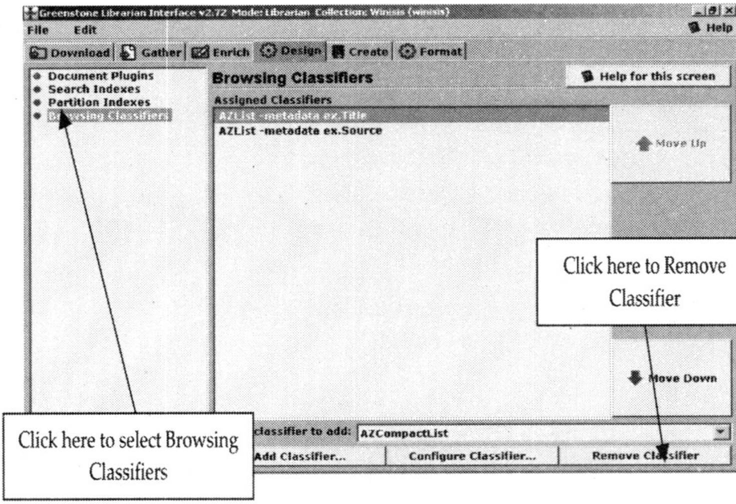


**Figure 10.14: Default Browsing Classifiers**

Select **Browsing Classifier** by clicking on it and then click on the **Remove Classifier** button for removing the default classifiers one by one. Default classifiers *ex.Title* and *ex.Source* are of no use in this case

The resultant screen would be as follows:-

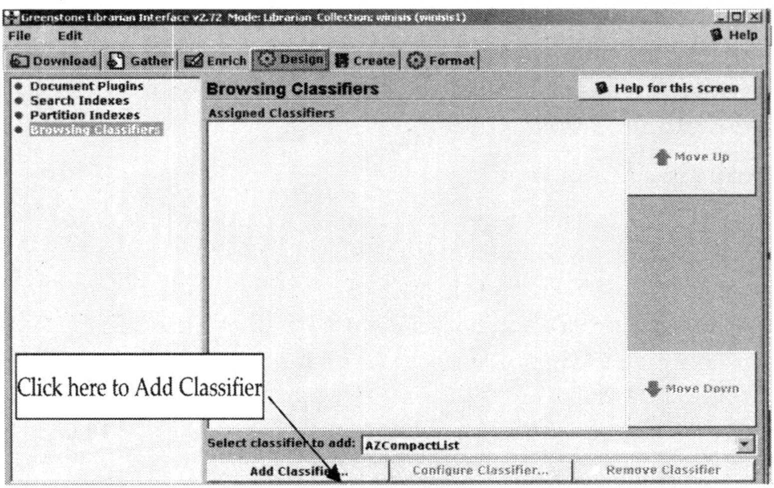


**Figure 10.15: Adding Classifier**

## Adding Browsing Classifiers

Now, choose **Select classifier to add** pull down list and select **A-Z List** or **A-Z Compact List**.

Use of AZCompactList Classifier brings bookshelf icons under the browsing classifier. It groups together the documents that appear multiple times with same metadata and does not differ with AZList in any other manner.

Then click on **Add Classifier** and add the Browsing Classifiers for **Title**, **Author** and **Keyword** by one by one.

If we want to give a button name other than the button names like **Titles, Creators** etc, check the buttonname box in the "Configuring Arguments" window, type the desired button name and click **Ok**.

When we click **Add Classifier** button in the above screen, we will get the window for choosing the **Browsing Classifier**.

Select the browsing classifier for *Title* by choosing the metadata option (exp.Title) as shown in Figure 10.16.

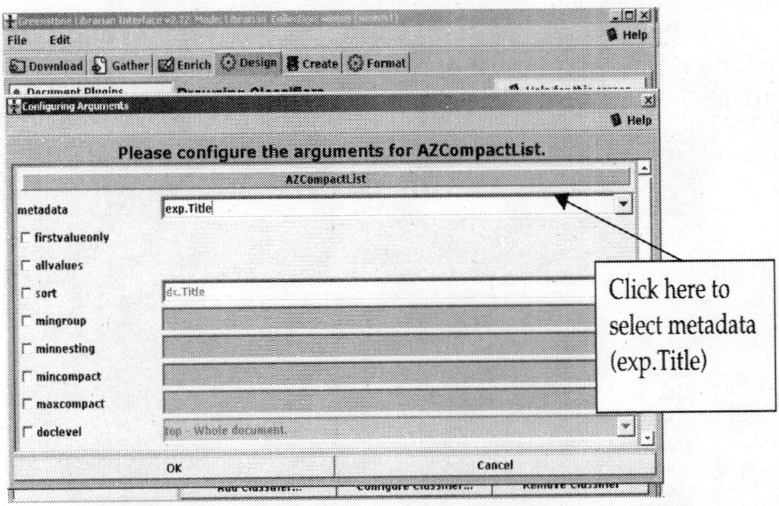


**Figure 10. 16: Adding Classifier CL1 for Title - exp.Title**

Click **OK** button to add *Title* classifier.

Then select the browsing classifier for *Author* by choosing the metadata option (exp.Author) as shown in Figure 10.17.

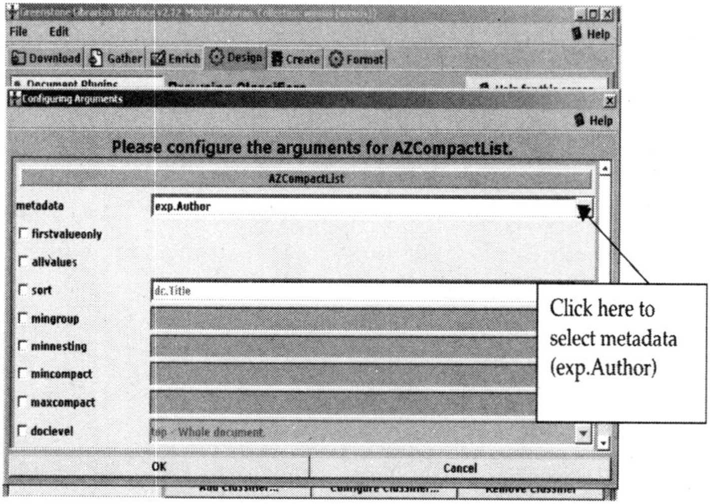


**Figure 10.17: Adding Classifier CL2 for Author - exp.Author**

Click **OK** button to add *Author* classifier.

Then select the browsing classifier for *Keyword* by choosing the metadata option (exp. Keyword) as in Figure 10.18.

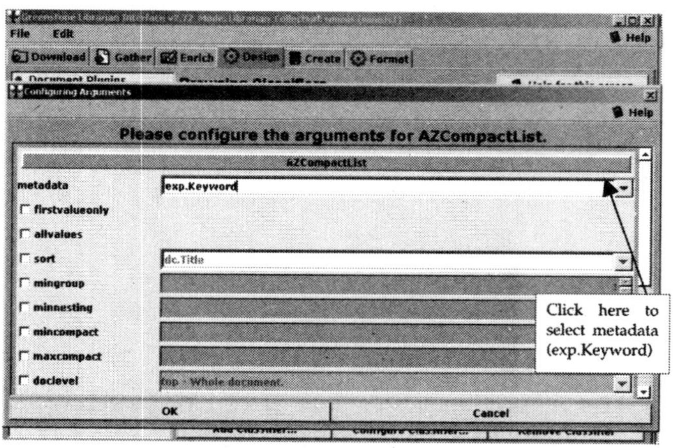


**Figure 10.18: Adding Classifier CL3 for Keywords**

Click **OK** button to add *Keyword* classifier.

The resultant screen, that shows the three added Browsing Classifiers, will appear as in Figure 10.19.

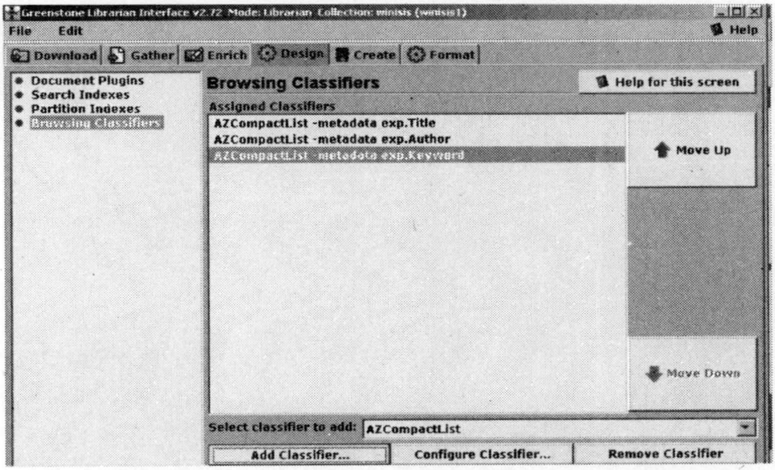


**Fig 10.19: Browsing Classifiers assigned for the Demo Collection**

## Format

Many aspects of the page-display of the resultant digital library are governed by the features provided under the **Format** menu.

## General

Choose the **Format** Tab and select **General** to provide the general information about the collection.

### Put a picture as a collection icon

Choose a small picture of around *100*100* pixels that needs to appear as an icon of the collection in the homepage, by clicking on the **Browse** button on middle right and selecting the picture. On choosing the picture, the fullpath of the picture will appear in the address box lying against the **Browse** button. We can provide the same picture or a different picture as the image for the 'about page' also. About page is the first page about an individual digital library collection that may contain a short description about the collection.

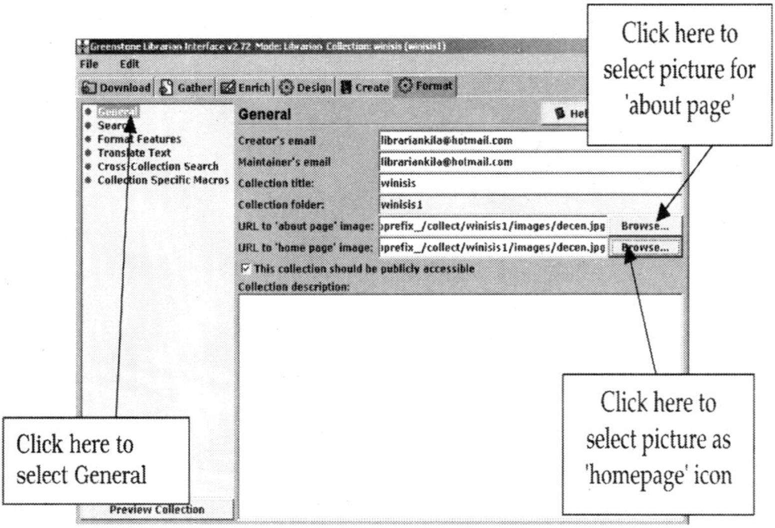


**Figure 10.20: Designing the Collection – General Information**

## Format Features

There are two types of Format Statements - General statement applicable in general to all and specific statement applicable to specific classifier or search list. Specific statements, if present, would override the general statements.

Let us examine some statements

VList - applies to all vertical lists in all classifiers

Search VList - applies to all search result lists

CL2HList - applies to all hierarchy lists in classifier 2

The value of any metadata can be interpolated by placing the metadata name in square brackets. eg. [Title] in the format statements.

[link] [icon] [/ link] provides a link from icon to the HTML version of the document.

[link] [Title] [/link] provides link from the Title of the document.

[srclink] [srcicon] [/srclink] provides a link from the word/pdf icon to the word/pdf version of the document.

**Format Features** allow unlimited choices in modifying the display features of the collection. Click on the **Format Features** section of the **Format** panel on the left pane as in Figure 10.21.

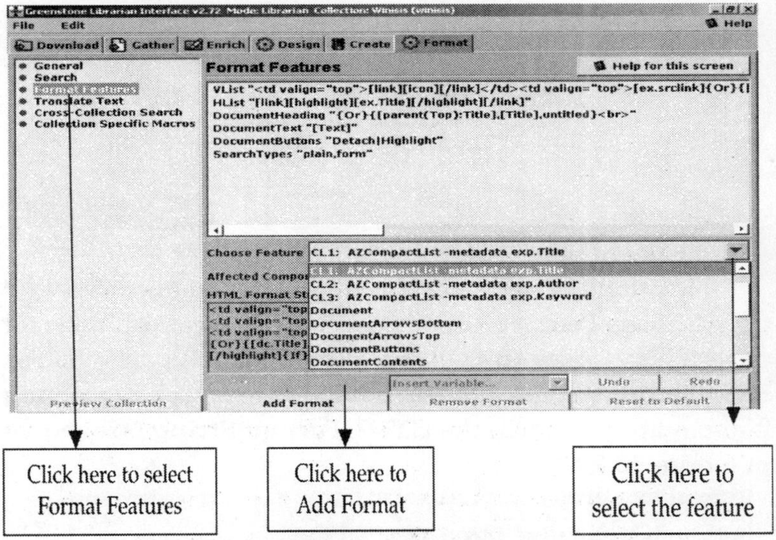


**Figure 10.21: Modifying the Format Features**

If we want to change any format feature, select the appropriate one (eg. CL1 AZCompactList- metadata exp.Title) from the **Choose Feature** pull down list and add the format string to the **Format Features** box by clicking on the **Add Format** button. You can select any feature appropriate for changing the display of the pages in the digital library. Fresh users may find it difficult to learn the format features in the beginning stage. But if properly understood, it is so easy to manage. The CL1 Browsing Classifier for Title can be added as shown in the following screen.

CL1 denotes the first browsing classifier exp.Title and CL2 denotes the second one exp.Author and so on.

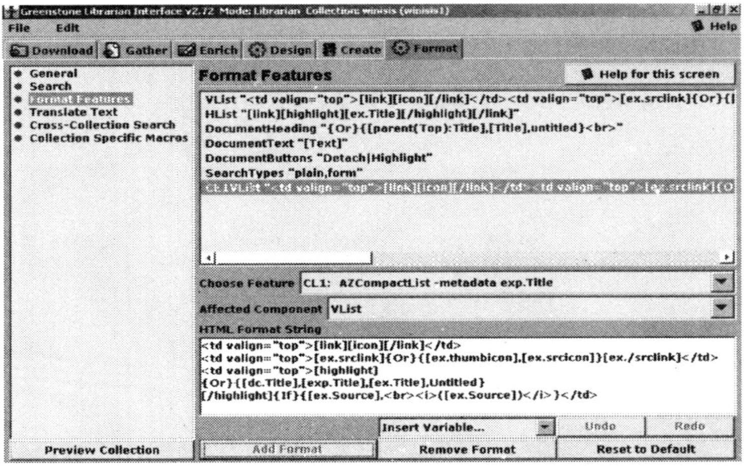

**Figure 10.22: Adding CL1 Browsing Classifier for exp.Title**

Similarly select other classifiers **Author** and **Keyword** from **Choose Feature** box and click **Add Format** button for customizing it as in the above screen. We can edit the HTML strings under the **Format Features** box by selecting it and editing them in the **HTML Format String** box shown in Figure 10.23.

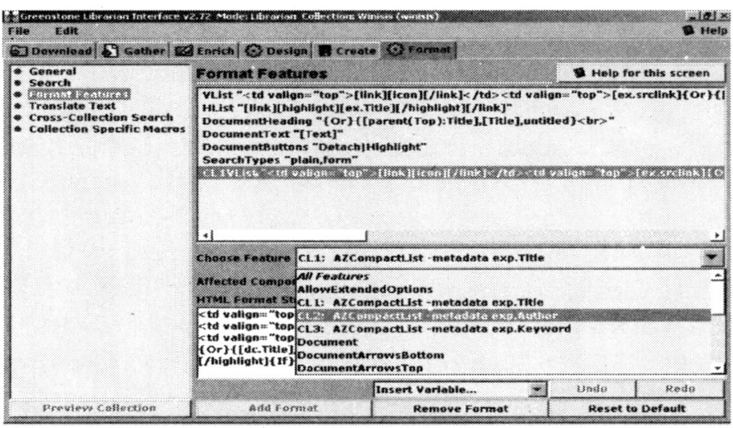

**Figure 10.23: Adding CL2 Browsing Classifier for exp.Author**

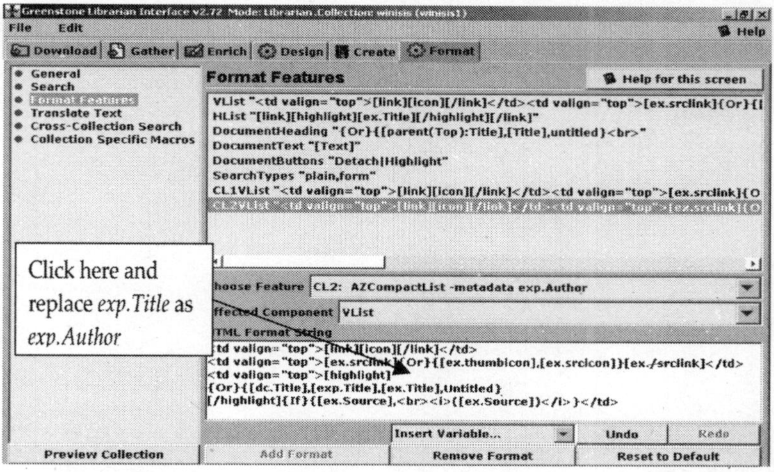


**Figure 10.24: Modifying the Format for exp.Author**

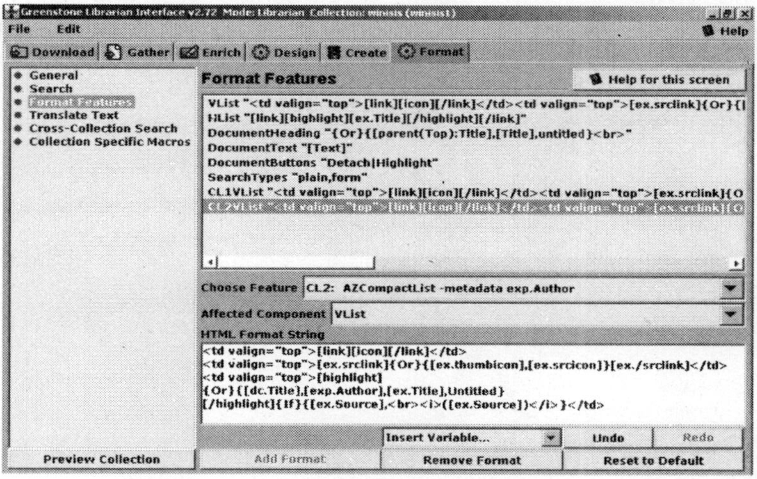


**Figure 10.25: Modified Format for exp.Author**

To add format feature for **Author** select the **CL2: AZCompactList-metadata exp.Author** in the **Choose Feature** and then click on the **Add Format** button. Then change in the **HTML Format String** *exp.Title* as *exp.Author*

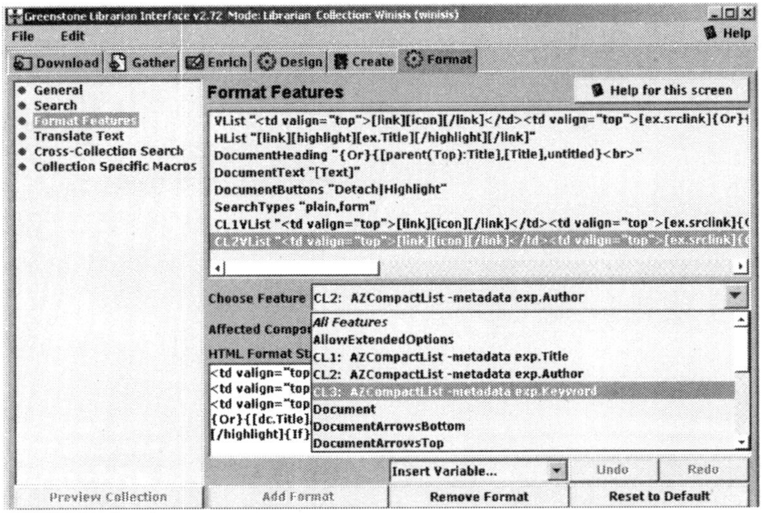

**Figure 10.26: Adding CL3 Browsing Classifier for exp.Keyword**

Choose the **CL3: AZCompactList-metadata exp.Keyword** and then add it by clicking on **Add Format** button.

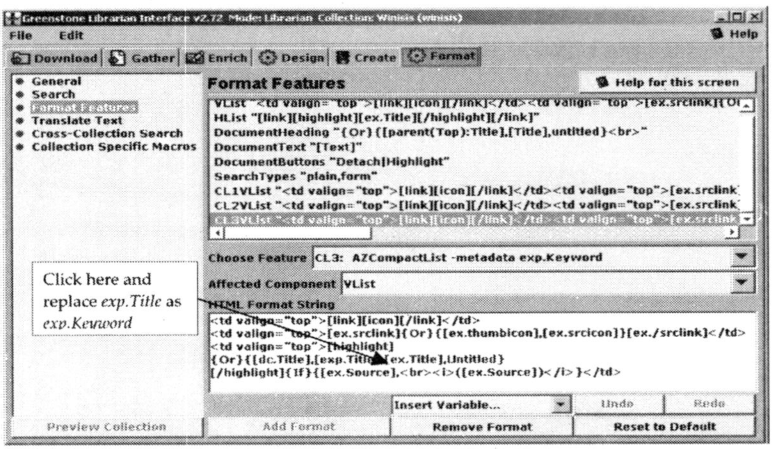


**Figure 10.27: Modifying the Format for exp.Keyword**

Then change the *exp.Title* as *exp.Keyword* as follows:-

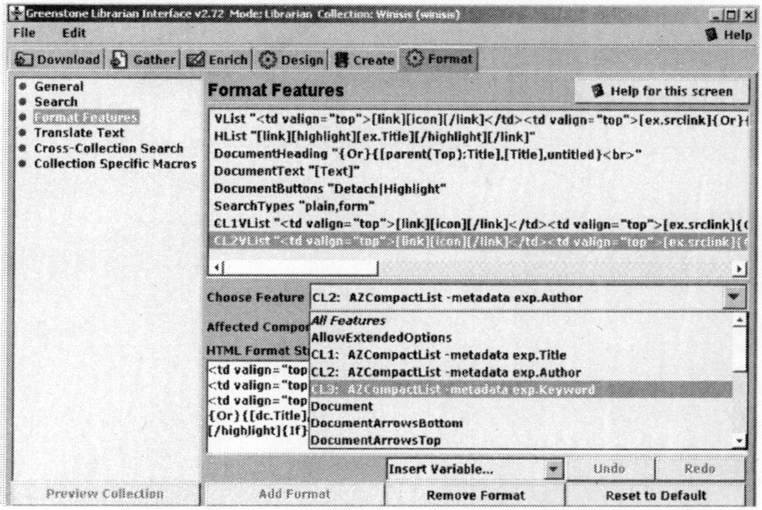

**Figure 10.28: Modified Format for exp.Keyword**

## Build the Collection

Then go to the **Create** panel. Click on the **Build Collection** button and the progress- window will show the progress in building the collection.

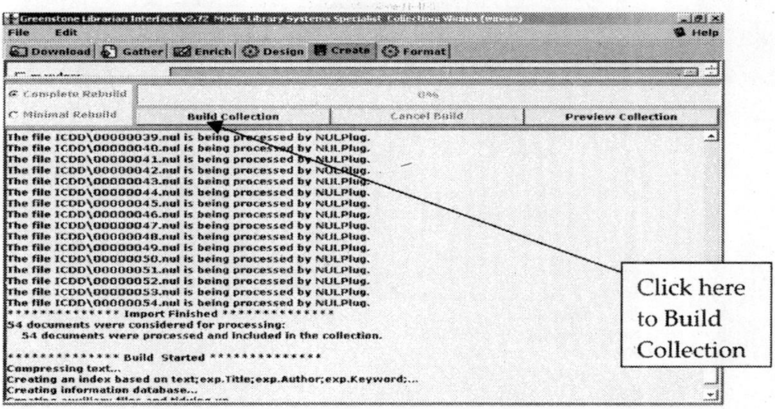


**Figure 10.29: Building a Collection**

## 2.5.1. Preview the Collection

At the end of the building process, Click on the **Preview Collection** button to view the collection built.

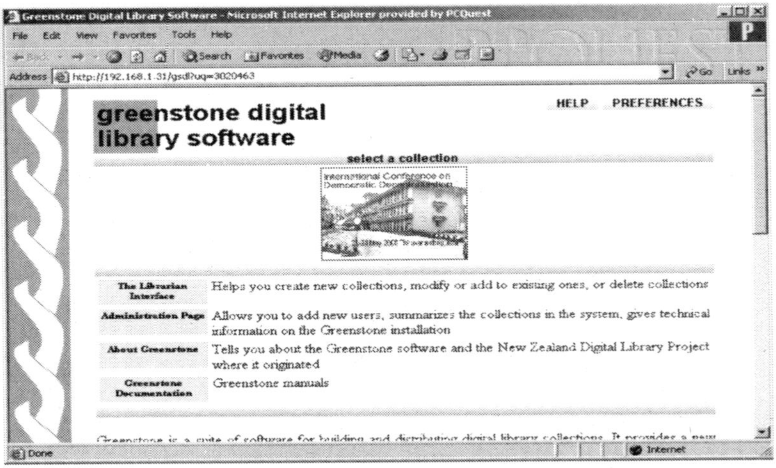


**Figure 10.30: Home Page of the Demo Collection**

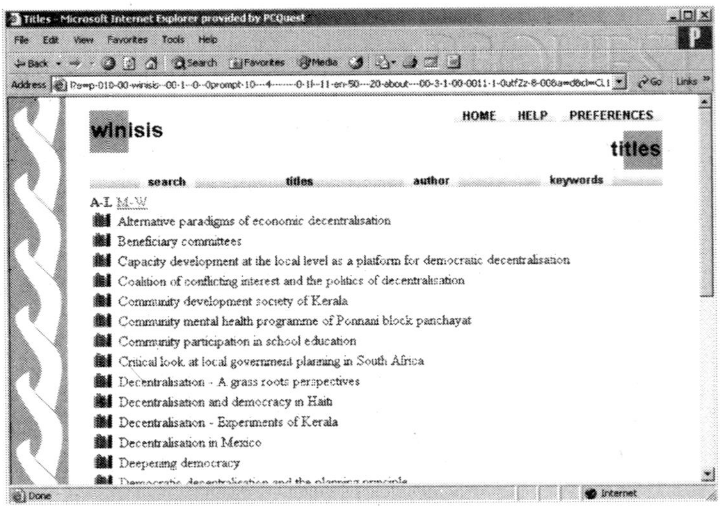


**Fig 10.31: Browse the Collection by Title Classifier**

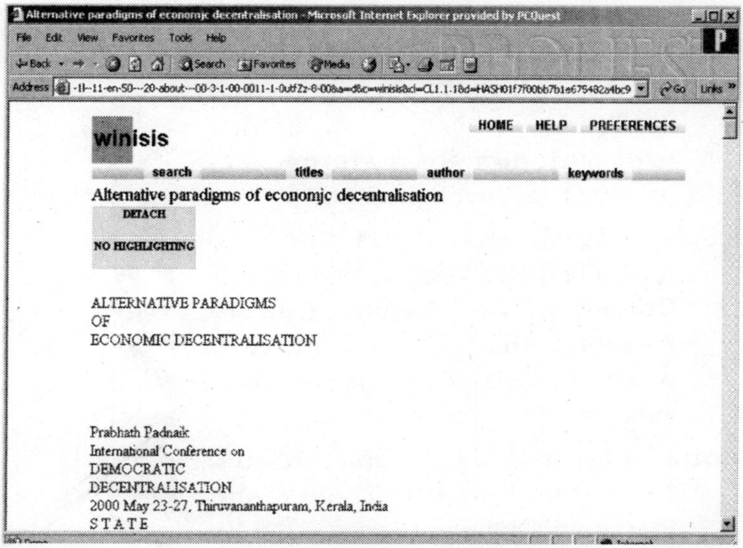

**Fig 10.32: Open the Full text Document**

# FURTHER READING & REFERENCES


Brainbridge, David et al (2004): Greenstone Digital Library Developer's Guide. New Zealand Digital Library Project, New Zealand. http://prdownloads.sourceforge.net/greenstone/Develop-en.pdf

Deepika Talagala. Web Interface for CDS/ISIS: GENISISWeb. Version 3.0.0. Colombo, Sri Lanka Library Association, 2004. http://www.nsf.ac.lk/purna/genisisman-ver.3.pdf

Digital Libraries'94 : First Annual Conference on the Theory and Practice of Digital Libraries. June 19-21, 1994, College Station, Texas.

Loots, M. et al (2001) From Paper to Collection. New Zealand Digital Library Project, New Zealand. http://prdownloads.sourceforge.net/greenstone/Paper-en.pdf

Morete, Pablo and Rose, John: Creating Digital Libraries Based on CDS/ISIS Databases. http://greenstone support.iimk.ac.in/Documents/CDS-ISIS_to_DL.pdf

Rajasekharan, K. (2005) Management of Digital Collections with WINISIS and Other Information Technologies. KELPRO Bulletin 9(1-2):pp. 17-32.

Rajasekharan, K. and Nafala, K. M. (2007) Building up a Digital Library with

Greenstone: a Self-Instructional Guide for Beginner's. Guide/Manual. http://eprints.rclis.org/archive/00009023/

Rajasekharan, K. and Nafala, K. M. (2007) Converting a WINISIS library Catalogue into a Greenstone Digital Library Application ("as is" conversion) . Guide/ Manual. http://eprints.rclis.org/archive/00010081/

Rajasekharan, K. and Nafala, K. M. (2007) Creating a Greenstone Digital Library with WINISIS Database. Guide/Manual. http://eprints.rclis.org/archive/00009024/

Rajasekharan, K. and Nafala, K. M. (2007) Creating Digital Document Archives with WINISIS & GenISISWeb Software. Guide/Manual. http://eprints.rclis.org/archive/00009027/

Rajasekharan, K. and Nafala, K. M. (2007) Creation of Digital Document Archives with WINISIS. Guide/Manual. http://eprints.rclis.org/archive/00009026/

Rajasekharan, K. and Nafala, K. M. (2007) Easy Ways to Customize the Display of Greenstone Pages. Guide/ Manual.

Rajasekharan, K. and Nafala, K. M. (2007) Manual for Creation of CD-ROM Library with GenisisCD/ GenisisCD. Guide/Manual. http://eprints.rclis.org/archive/00009031/

Rajasekharan, K. and Nafala, K. M. (2007) Manual on digital document archiving. Guide/Manual. http://eprints.rclis.org/archive/00009029/

Raman Nair, R. Basics of CDS/ISIS for DOS. New Delhi, Ess Ess, 1998.

Raman Nair, R. Computer application to library and information services, New Delhi, Ess Ess, 1990.

Tutorial exercises on Greenstone at http://

greenstone.sourceforge.net/wiki/ index.php/ Tutorial_exercises

UNESCO. CDS/ISIS for Windows Handbook. Paris, UNESCO, 2004.

UNESCO. WINISIS 1.5 Reference Manual. Paris, UNESCO, 2004.

Witten, Ian H and Boddie, Stefan (2004): Greenstone Installer's Guide. http://downloads.sourceforge.net/ greenstone/Install-en.pdf. New Zealand Digital Library Project, New Zealand

Witten, Ian H and Boddie, Stefan (2004): Greenstone Installer's Guide. New Zealand Digital Library Project, New Zealand. http://prdownloads. sourceforge.net/ greenstone/Install-en.pdf

Witten, Ian H and Brainbridge, David (2003) : How to build a digital library. http://www.nzdl.org/custom/howto/ collect/howto/pdf/FrontMatter.pdf. Amsterdam, Morgan Kaufmann

Witten, Ian. H. et al (2006) Greenstone User's Guide. New Zealand Digital Library Project, New Zealand. http:/ /prdownloads.sourceforge.net/greenstone/User-en.pdf

Witten, Ian.H. et al (2006) Greenstone User's Guide. http:/ /greenstonesupport.iimk.ac.in/Documents/ Users_Guide.pdf) New Zealand Digital Library Project, New Zealand.

# GLOSSARY

**Analogue** Descriptive data represented as a continuous variable, such as sound or an electrical impulse.

**Apache** A free web server run in around 70 percent of the websites

**Application** A computer programme designed for a particular use, such as a word processor, database management system etc.

**Client/Server mode** A computer network model where the client- *a web server*- places a request and the server- *a web server*- serves the pages requested

**Cybrarian** A librarian or researcher specializing in the Internet, rather than books, as a source of information

**Database** An application used to store and manipulate data

**Digital** Represented by a distinct value, as the 0 or 1 of a binary computer system

**Digitalization** is a process of turning a physical form of document into a computer readable format. Digitalization requires a scanner and an optical character recognition (OCR) software

**Ftp** is file transfer protocol. It is a protocol used to upload or download files kept in ftp sites. You can upload/download information from an ftp site with a web browser

**Home page** A page that acts like a front door to the content of the website

**Http** is the short form for *hypertext transfer*

*protocol*. It is a language or set of rules used to communicate between a server and browser

**IP address** The address of a particular computer in a network, which have four groups of three digit numbers, ranging from 0 to 255. (eg. http://100.0.0.60)

**LAN** Local Area Network. Tow or more computers that are linked within an office or a building to share programs, data, output, devices etc.

**Link** is a highlighted word that has a connection to a target page and a click on the link will open the target page

**MP3** is a compressed sound file meant for electronic distribution and it occupies only 10 percent of .wav sound files

**OCR** is a process of turning a scanner image into a computer editable text, so that the text can be retyped manually

**PDF** Portable Document Format is suitable format for publishing in Internet and distribute documents through e-mail

**Protocol** A set of commands/rules that determine how two computers communicate with each other. http, ftp, TCP/IP etc are common protocols used in Internet

**Query** Any request for information from a database

**Query form** is a submit form where you can type a query

**TCP/IP** is the short form for Transfer Control Protocol & Internet Protocol. This protocol governs the sending of data from one computer to another computer in Internet or a local network

**Upload** Transferring information from a local computer to a remote web server across a network

**Web Browser** software is used for viewing WebPages. It is needed to display the pages held in a web server.

Internet explorer is the most popular web server.

**Web server** is a computer in the Internet that stores websites and serves the documents stored in the computer on search requests made through a web browser.

**Website** A location in the World Wide Web identified by a web address such as www.kilaonline.org. Websites are stored in web servers.

**Window** A rectangular viewing area on a computer monitor screen where data is displayed.

**Windows** A menu driven graphical user interface in which programs, directories and files are indicated by icons, and data is displayed in rectangular frames that can be manipulated by the user.

SOFTWARE CDROM

The attached CDROM contains all the software packages covered by this manual. It is to be used only along with the book for training purposes. Even though all are Open Source or free packages users are requested to download latest versions from concerned sites and follow the terms and conditions mentioned by the developers before actually using these packages for developing permanent digital libraries, archives or Institutional Repositories.

When the CDROM is inserted into the CDDRIVE if Auto run facility of the computer is enabled the following home page of the CDROM will automatically get opened.

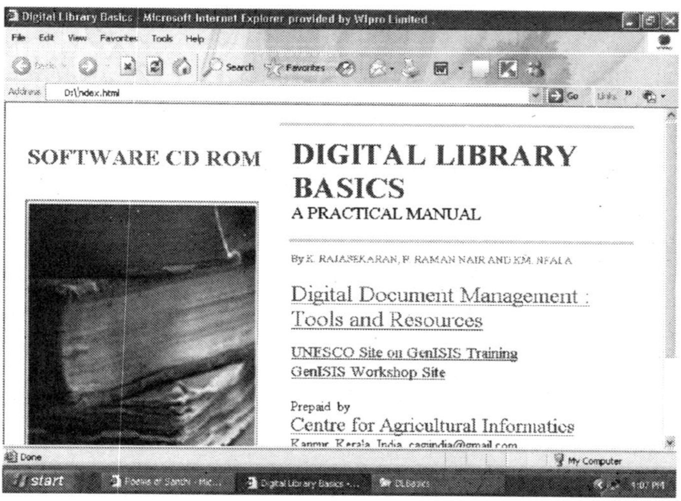


If the home page of the CDROM is not getting opened automatically we can go to the CD Drive in Windows Explorer and double click the file **index.html** in the CDROM drive. Then the home page of the CDROM will come to the Screen.

By clicking the first sub head in the page entitled ' Digital Document Management Tools and Resources' we can go to the section containing the software packages.

By double clicking the UNESCO site on GenISIS Training we can reach the page in UNESCO site where information about training on GenISIS related packages are provided by UNESCO.

By double clicking the option GenISIS workshop site we can reach the web pages providing information on Gen ISIS training in India.

By clicking the first sub head in the page entitled 'Digital Document Management tools and Resources' the following page containing the software packages and detailed manuals for each package required for practising and reference will get opened.

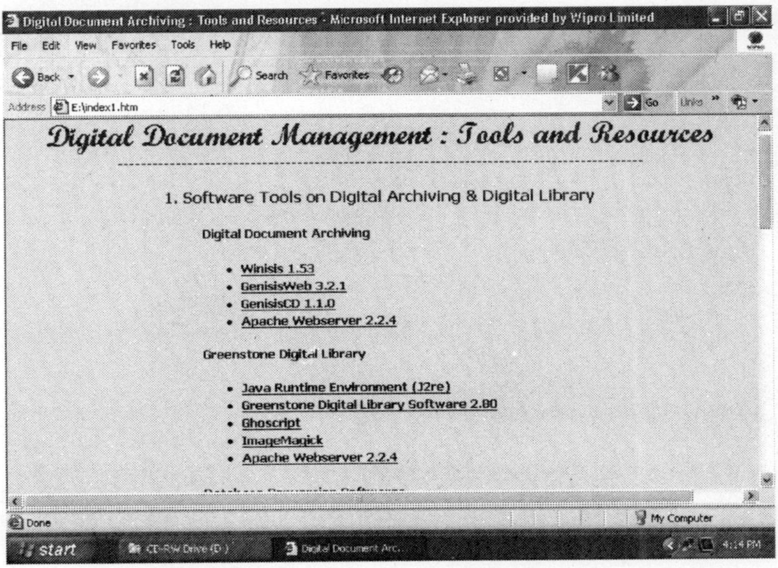

By clicking the concerned package users can install the package in the computer. By clicking the concerned manual users can get the detailed manual on the package.